Th

Valley 101

Great Big Book of Life

by Clay Thompson

PRIMER
PUBLISHERS

Phoenix, Arizona

Primer Publishers
5738 North Central Avenue
Phoenix, Arizona 85012
www.claythompsonbooks.com
info@primerpublishers.com
(800) 521-9221

Cover design by ATG Productions, Inc., Christy Moeller-Masel — www.atgproductions.com
Interior design by The Printed Page, Lisa Liddy — www.theprintedpage.com
Printed by Central Plains Book Manufacturing, Winfield, KS — www.centralplainsbook.com

ISBN 0-935810-73-0

Publisher's Cataloging-In-Publication Data
(Prepared by The Donohue Group, Inc.)

Thompson, Clay.
    The valley 101 : great big book of life / by Clay Thompson.

     p. cm.
    ISBN: 0-935810-73-0

1. Questions and answers. 2. Questions and answers -- Humor. 3. Curiosities and wonders. I. Title.

AG195 .T86 2005
031/.02

For Robert and Eleanor
My parents

Contents

Assorted oddities... 143

Foreword

My friend Clay Thompson has gone and done it again. If books were babies, Planned Parenthood would be coming down on him to practice more restraint. Clay's daily column in the *Arizona Republic* is the first thing I, and many other Arizonans, check each day, and now he's turned them into another wonderfully entertaining book. These are questions that most people would be afraid to ask. And no matter how dumb, Clay handles them with a finesse that is reminiscent of a Don Rickles lounge show.

Not surprisingly, there are lots of questions about the weather. There are times here in Arizona when there isn't much else to talk about. And there is such a diversity of weather in the state. We often have the hottest and coldest national temperatures on the same day. It's so dry in western Arizona the cows give powdered milk, and so hot in southern Arizona people get third degree burns in their swimming pools. It's so cold in Flagstaff that the flashers will only describe themselves. Yup, weather is a favorite topic out here.

Did you ever wonder what a "Ruth Party" was? A clue: It has nothing to do with the famous trunk murderess.

There's a lot of other useful information in this newest Valley 101 too, like what to do with your Bermuda grass in the winter time. Does eating hot, spicy foods in the summer cool us down or do they make us hotter? And why are there so few tall buildings in Arizona? My personal favorites were Clay's reflections on harvester ants mating in the swimming pool, why do dogs love to roll in smelly things like duck poop, and how to get javalinas to stop pooping in your yard. That says a lot about me, too, but you can see there's a lot of handy information here.

Much of Clay's humor is directed towards new arrivals to the state and that's not unusual. After all, Arizona is a land of anomalies and tamales. We have birds that run faster than they fly, flowers that bloom only at night, bark scorpions that don't bark, and an entire forest that got stoned. All of New England plus Pennsylvania and Delaware would easily fit inside our borders. The town of Maricopa is in Pinal County; Gila Bend is in Maricopa County; Pima is in Graham County; Fort Apache's in Navajo County and Navajo is in Apache County. No wonder our newcomers are confused.

There's also some useful information that every Arizonan should know, such as the legal description of the Mogollon Rim, and why does Arizona have that weird diagonal line on her southern border between Nogales and the Colorado River. My favorite was the story of Wallace, Ladmo, and Gerald. If you have to ask who they were, we're going to have to revoke your Arizona citizenship papers.

Did you ever see plastic foam cups placed on cactus during cold weather? Did you think they were Christmas decorations? Do we have quicksand in Arizona? I've always wondered why those stagecoach wheels in western movies appeared to be going backwards. Have you ever been told that your hair grows faster in hot weather? We know that hot weather makes people stick together but does white clothing keep us cooler than black? Read the book and find out.

Marshall Trimble
Official Arizona State Historian

Acknowledgments

I am tempted here just to acknowledge myself. Something like, "Way to go, Clay. You've managed to snooker *The Republic* into paying you just for sitting around having a great time doing the Valley 101 column. Sweet."

I suppose that wouldn't be very good form. And, besides, they don't pay me all that much.

So I made a list of all the people I should thank for their help and support, advice and encouragement. Then I studied on the list for a bit and I realized that a lot of those people are decent, upright folks, respected in their communities, who might not want their names associated with a low-rent operation like Valley 101. So I have decided not to name names.

So I am going to weenie out and just give a collective thanks to everyone involved. You know who you are, and you know I couldn't do it without you. (OK, I'll name one name: Thanks, Annie, and good luck. All the best.)

As always, though, my deepest appreciation goes to the people who read the column and for whatever reason seem to enjoy it. Thanks. You guys remind me every day just how interesting people are. And how odd.

All creatures great and small and some plants and stuff...

Some people say God made the world and everything in it in seven days. Well, six days plus the day of rest. Some people say it was a process that took billions of years, but God was the mastermind behind it. Some people say God didn't have anything to do with it and it was something that just sort of happened over billions of years, the world and the plants and bugs and other animals and all that.

Myself, I try not to worry about it. I figure if God was involved and wants us to know just exactly how he did it, he'll tell us in his own good time. If he wasn't involved, we'll just have to try to figure it out ourselves. Until one or the other happens, I believe I'll just mow the lawn and maybe take a nap afterwards and more or less wait and be surprised. I'm thinking that if God does call a news conference and make some surprise announcement about how he or she did or didn't do it, it will be in the paper the next day.

Anyway, I think this section — the part about plants and bugs and other animals and so forth — is my favorite part of this book. That's because it reminds me what a wonderful and odd and amazing world we live in and how many wonderful and odd and amazing things there are all around us. That one about the big gob of stuff thrashing around in the guy's swimming pool and it turned out to be a bunch of ants bent on procreation? That was really something.

I suppose the point, if there is one, is that we have to pay attention. There's all this swell stuff out there that needs looking at and wondering about and it's not all gigantic three-toed yak-eating lizards from far-off Bingo-Bongo Land like you might read about in *National Geographic* or something like that. It's stuff that's right under your nose. Like those amorous ants or the dog with smelly ears or how Bermuda grass reproduces or bobbing birds or some such stuff.

So I think it's all really something. Of course, it helps to be not very bright, because then almost everything is really something. It's like a great quote I read once about dogs, and I can't remember who said it. It was something like this: Every time a dog walks into a room, it's surprised.

Well, every time I listen to my messages or check the e-mails or open up the Valley 101 mailbag, I'm surprised. I'm surprised at the things you people wonder about and surprised that I didn't wonder about them before myself and surprised at how interesting the answers are. But then as I said, being dim helps.

Dog's Ears Need Trip To The Vet

October 28, 2000

Q: *Why do my golden retriever's ears stink in the fall?*

A: It may be tempting fate to say this, but we believe this may be the single greatest question we have ever received at Valley 101.

When this question arrived, the entire Valley 101 staff gathered around and stared at it for some time in mute appreciation. Its simplicity and elegance are breathtaking. The sweep of its weirdness is stunning. There is talk of having it framed, or at least laminated.

We bow to you, madam; nay, kneel in humble gratitude that you have bestowed upon us this great gift.

It almost seems a shame to answer such a masterpiece, but answer it we must:

Your dog's sick, lady.

We have reached this conclusion after conferring with a number of experts, including the guy in the next cubicle who has a whole bunch of golden retrievers.

Old Fido probably has an ear infection. Dogs, we are told, are especially prone to this sort of thing in the summer, especially if they're fond of swimming.

The guy in the next cubicle thinks his dogs get it from swimming in his neighbor's pool. If we were his neighbor, we would be a little concerned about a diseased dog swimming in our pool, but he didn't say anything about that.

So anyway, your dog's ears get water in them and one thing leads to another, and pretty soon Rover has an ear infection and pretty soon it starts to smell.

You don't even want to think about what it looks like in there. You should take the pooch to a veterinarian some time soon.

All this brings to mind one of our favorite jokes, the world-famous schnauzer joke, which now resides under lock and key in the official Valley 101 Vault and Yogurt Storage Unit on the advice of our attorneys.

In Tribute To Spiders' Crafty Ways
July 5, 2001

Why don't spiders get caught in their own webs?

Well, because they just don't, do they? What would be the point of God inventing spiders and having them spin webs if they ended up getting caught in them?

Nonetheless, I put your question to David Maddison, associate professor of entomology at the University of Arizona, and he said he didn't know and, besides, I had him mixed up with his twin brother, Wayne, who also teaches at UA and knows all about spiders. But Wayne was out of town.

David, however, was nice enough to steer me in the right direction, and I eventually arrived at an answer. It may even actually be a correct answer.

Most spiders have at the ends of their feet something called "walking claws" that allow the spider to get a firm grip of smooth surfaces such as leaves or grass. In front of these claws is a hooked third claw surrounded by bent hairs with lots of spines. The spider uses these claws to grasp the silk lines of its web and move along them without getting caught.

Some spiders also have an oily covering on their bodies that lets them move around the sticky parts of the web without getting bogged down.

As long as we're on the subject, did you know spiders don't have any muscles in their legs? They move them by raising or lowering their blood pressure.

Spider silk is actually kind of cool. On the basis of weight, it is stronger than steel, and it has been said that a strand of spider silk the thickness of a pencil could stop a Boeing 747 in flight. I don't suppose anybody is ever going to test that out.

Silk is produced as a liquid that hardens as it leaves the spider's spinnerets. Spiders have from one to four spinnerets that can contain as many as 50,000 small tubes.

And spiders have different glands that release different fluids depending on what the silk will be used for — stickiness, wrapping egg sacs, wrapping prey, etc.

Did you know that there is a kind of spider that can catch small fish? That's gross.

An Ant Orgy? In My Pool? Oh, Yuck!

July 28, 2001

Recently I noticed some black puffballs or seedpods floating in the swimming pool. I tossed one on to the edge of the pool and looked at it closely, and it started moving. It was a bunch of ants hanging on to each other. When they had dispersed, there was absolutely nothing left. What was going on?

I guess your pleasure in having an answer depends on how you feel about other species reproducing in your swimming pool. The ants were having a bit of the old slap and tickle, so to speak.

They probably were carpenter or harvester ants, although it is hard to tell without seeing them firsthand, even for such an expert as the estimable entomologist Carl Olson of the University of Arizona. Olson is the co-author of *Insects of the Southwest*, which is one of my favorite books, especially if I can't get to sleep.

I do not mean to be snarky here. It is a well-written and useful book. It is interesting enough to hold the layperson's attention but not such a page-turner that it keeps you awake for more than a chapter or so. Plus the softcover edition won't rap the bridge of your nose if the book pitches forward on your face after you fall asleep. I recommend it highly.

Anyway, I consulted with Olson on your question, and he said this is the time of year when a young ant's fancy turns to procreation.

"We're in the throes of the mating season. Sex is on the wing, if you will," said he. "All sorts of ants are leaving the nest and flying away in clusters. What she saw was a big glob of ants, a mass of ant humanity, I suppose you could say."

This is the deal: If you knew how to tell the boy ants from the girl ants and if you had pried that glob of ants apart one by one, you probably would have found at the center one female ant, no doubt somewhat bedraggled, surrounded by a bunch of sex-crazed male ants, all vying for her attention, assuming ants have attention. It was, in Olson's words, "an ant orgy."

Water Bags Repel Flies, Not Masters

August 11, 2001

A couple of years ago we were sitting on our porch enjoying some beers, but not enjoying all the flies. A friend suggested hanging up plastic bags of water to repel the flies. We tried it, and it works, but we have never known why. What's the deal?

My first thought was that this was just about the most cocka-mamie idea I had ever heard, but then I looked at my pay stub and decided the water-bags thing didn't sound so weird after all.

Apparently there is something to this, but no one seems to know why.

The idea is this: Fill a sandwich-size, zip-top plastic bag about half full of water. A couple of references I found said you should mix in a bit of vinegar, too.

Hang the bag up, either with good old duct tape or by poking a wire hanger through the top. Supposedly, this repels flies.

I don't know this for sure, but I found a number of references that swore it works. I do know it does not work on my masters, but I have had some success in that area with those stop sticks the police put down to flatten the tires of cars they are chasing.

There are a couple of theories about why the water-bag thing works.

One holds that to flies the bags resemble hornets' nests, and since hornets prey on flies, the pests steer clear.

Maybe, maybe not.

Another explanation is that there is something about the way light reflects off the bags that somehow scares or confuses the fly. I know you can scare flies, but I don't know how hard it is to confuse flies. I don't recall ever having seen a confused fly.

Speaking of that, another reader wants to know: *How can flies see anything if they have hundreds of eyes? How could their tiny fly brains process all those images?*

Flies and other insects don't have thousands of eyes. They have thousands of lenses. You have two lenses that form a single image. Flies have thousands of lenses, but they form only one image. Don't ask me how they know this.

Oh, The Webs Many Spiders Will Weave

September 19, 2001

How do spiders build webs across long distances, like between two bushes a few feet apart?

Did you know that a few years ago scientists spliced some spider genes into a couple of goats in order to harvest spider silk from the goats' milk? That's kind of scary sounding, don't you think? It would be like splicing genes from some venomous reptile into one of my masters in order to create a better poison or weed killer or something.

Anyway, about your question: There are about a gazillion different kinds of spiders, and different spiders spin different kinds of webs. But their most common strategy for getting started is to churn out a long, sticky thread and let it float away on the breeze. When it sticks to something the spider crosses the span and reinforces it until it is sturdy enough to anchor the web. Then it sets about weaving the pattern of web that particular brand of spider uses.

If it's a busy night and the web takes a pounding, the spider will eat it up, except for the original bridge strand, and then weave a new web.

Did you know that scientists at NASA once did some experiments where they gave spiders stuff like caffeine and marijuana and tranquilizers to see what would happen?

Isn't that great? Don't you wish you were a scientist so you could sit around and think up cool experiments like that? The point of the experiment was to test the toxicity of new medicines, but I bet a bunch of guys at NASA just thought it might be fun to get a spider stoned. I wonder how they did that.

Anyway, the spiders on marijuana started spinning their webs, but lost interest about halfway through. The spiders on speed went at it with a lot of vim and vigor but spun webs with big holes in them. The spiders on caffeine made webs with deformed designs. And the spiders who took chloral hydrate, an ingredient in some sleeping pills, not surprisingly fell asleep.

Science marches on.

Tarantulas No Jumpers, Just Feelers

September 22, 2001

A friend at work told me that tarantulas can jump. Can they really? That creeps me out.

Jumping tarantulas? Oh, man, that's gross. That would be like seeing my masters naked — you don't even want to think about it.

Fortunately, this is not true. Tarantulas find their prey by touch and have poor eyesight. So there would be no point in jumping, aside from the possibility that it might be kind of funny to watch.

Your pal has confused tarantulas with jumping spiders, which turn out to be fairly interesting things.

Jumping spiders are of the family Salticidae that includes about 5,000 species. Salticidae comes from a Latin word for dance. This is because guy jumping spiders hit on girl jumping spiders by doing an elaborate dance.

Aside from the fact that they jump, the cool thing about jumping spiders is their eyes. They have four big eyes on their faces and four smaller eyes on the top of their heads. Don't ask me how they coordinate them. I don't know. However they do it, the eyesight of jumping spiders is thought to be as good as ours. They've even been known to watch television. Really.

All those eyes mean they can spot their prey from a fair distance. Then they creep up and jump on it. A jumping spider can leap about 50 times its body length, which is a pretty good trick. It does this by contracting the muscles in the front of its body to build up blood pressure, which causes its legs to extend rapidly. It shoots forward like one of those little toy frogs that hop when you squeeze the bulb. I wonder if they still make those.

There's another cool thing: Some jumping spiders grab their prey right out of the air. They spin out a line of silk, attach one end to a branch or something, and when the prey flies by, they swing out and grab it. If they miss, they climb back up the strand and wait for something else. That's neat. I wonder if they do little spider Tarzan yells when they swing out there.

Carob Trees Rank Among The Rankest
November 25, 2001

Today's question: *Our neighbor has two carob trees. Every November in the late afternoon or evening, just when I go to relax on my patio, the most horrific odor wafts through the neighborhood. It smells like a laundry bin at the Y. Why?*

You're living next door to two carob trees? Oh, man you are sooooo out of luck. Various sources I checked used words or phrases such as: "fetid," "Limburger cheese," "malodorous," "rotting carcass" and "unendurable" to describe the smell of carob pods.

Carobs smell so bad because the pods have a 1.3 percent isobutyric acid content. You know how rancid butter smells? That's because of the butyric acid in it, and isobutyric acid is almost the same thing. It stinks.

What I haven't been able to figure out is if there is some survival reason for this; if the smell is meant to attract or repel some thing or things.

Aside from the smell, carobs are kind of interesting. They are natives of the Mediterranean area, do fairly well here and are good shade trees.

Our word carat, as in the unit of weight for gems, comes from the word carob because carob seeds were once used for weighing precious stones. Five carob seeds weigh about 1 gram.

In ancient times, carob husks were sold as livestock food or sustenance for the poor, who ate them plain or boiled them into a kind of molasses. Today, of course, it is a chocolate substitute.

Some scholars think that it was carob husks that John the Baptist was eating when the Bible speaks of him living in the wilderness and subsisting on "locusts and wild honey." Hence, carobs are also known as locust trees or St. John's bread. When the Prodigal Son was reduced to working as a swineherd and sharing the "husks" the pigs ate, it was probably carob.

As to how to deal with the smell, I have two plans: leave town every November or buy your neighbor's house and cut down the trees.

Other than that, as noted above, you are out of luck. And why were you smelling the laundry bin at the Y, anyway?

Why Dogs Seem To Love Smelly Stuff

November 27, 2001

Why do dogs insist on rolling around in poop or other foul-smelling stuff? I've had to give my dog three baths in two days.

The quick and easy and most logical answer is that your dog is a moron. Many of them are. However, this is not the correct answer.

There are, it turns out, a number of possible answers. Most of them are associated with ancient, deeply ingrained animal instincts, dating back to time immemorial when our ancestors lived in trees and cowered at night to the howls of great packs of free-ranging schipperkes. One theory is that some stuff that smells foul to us smells good to dogs. Who knows? A dog might enjoy the smell of a big pile of duck poop as much as you enjoy the smell of freshly baked bread. Don't you think that would make a great perfume? Freshly baked bread, that is.

Another idea is that rolling around in a carcass or droppings was a way to convey a message back to the rest of the pack. Sort of like saying: "Look what I found!" Of course, you would think the rest of the pack would say, "You found moose poop? What a moron." But I guess it didn't work that way.

Yet another theory holds that rolling in foul stuff was a way of disguising the dog's own smell, either to cover it up as the dog sneaked up on prey or to mask it from predators. I suppose that works.

Of course, you could probably cut down on the problem by keeping your yard clean of droppings or dead things or by keeping your dog on a leash when you walk it. Or you can try aversive action. Did you know you can buy a training collar that sprays citronella by remote control? Dogs hate the smell of citronella.

Or you can carry around a coffee can or something with a handful of pennies in it and shake it vigorously when it looks like the hound is about to dive into some wretched substance. The dog will be scared by the noise. I know I am.

Cucumbers Are Cool — Here's Why
December 5, 2001

Why do cucumbers taste and feel cool even though they may be at room temperature?

Hmm.... That's a good question, and as it turns out, there is a perfectly logical answer, which I know will come as a surprise to regular readers.

I found several sources that said the inside of a cucumber can be as much as 20 degrees cooler than the outside, but I could not find an explanation for this. That's because it turned out to be a lot of hooey.

A cucumber that was 20 degrees cooler than its surroundings would be in violation of the First Law of Thermodynamics, also known as the Law of Conservation of Energy. I do not actually know the first thing about this law, but that's what it said in *What Einstein Didn't Know*, an excellent book by Robert Wolke, a chemistry professor at the University of Pittsburgh.

Wolke points out that if the insides of a cucumber were really 20 degrees cooler than its surroundings, it would be constantly throwing off heat in order to stay cool. If it were constantly throwing off heat, we wouldn't need electricity or oil to power stuff. We could harness the awesome power of the cucumber. We could build cucumber bombs. And we probably would.

Do this: Leave a cucumber and a rutabaga on the counter for several hours. Cut them and hold the sliced surfaces to your forehead. They're both going to feel cool. Duh. That's because they're at room temperature, which is say, 72 degrees, and you're at person temperature: 98.6 degrees.

Cucumbers, by the way, are thought to be among the first plants cultivated by people. They are about 96 percent water; perhaps that enhances the sensation of coolness. They also have a lot of potassium, vitamin A, vitamin C and some silicone. Maybe that's why they are good for your skin.

So, after your experiment, eat the cucumber. Throw away the rutabaga. I wouldn't eat a rutabaga on a bet.

Yes, Birds Can Have Heart Attacks

December 22, 2001

Today's question: *Do birds have heart attacks? If so, has anyone ever been hurt by a stricken bird falling from the sky?*

You know, I'm thinking maybe it's time to take a break, a little R&R. Questions like this age a person. Maybe I'll go fishing. Maybe I'll just sit around in my bathrobe for a few days and look up goofy stuff on the Internet. Wait, that's what I'm doing now. I'll think of something.

Birds have hearts. Ergo, birds can have heart attacks. And it turns out they have heart attacks for some of the same reasons people do. Stress and unhealthy diets, to name a few.

Last year the European Scientific Committee on Animal Health and Animal Welfare reported that worldwide about 5 percent of the broilers raised in those big factory chicken farms die of heart attacks.

The birds grow so quickly in the factory conditions that their hearts and lungs can't keep up with the rest of their bodies and — kerplop — they drop dead from heart attacks. And chickens are not good candidates for CPR.

Pet birds, such as parrots or canaries or whatever, also are susceptible. Even a loud noise can bring on a heart attack in little birds. That's why you shouldn't put a bird cage too close to the TV. A good, noisy shoot-em-up comes on and it's goodbye, Tweetie.

Parrots have been known to topple over from getting their beaks or toenails trimmed. And since parrots eat a lot of fatty foods such as sunflower seeds or peanuts, their arteries can get clogged up just like yours would on a diet of double cheeseburgers. Flaxseed is said to be a good counter to high-fat diets.

One assumes that in-the-wild birds are getting a lot of exercise flying around and stuff and eating healthy foods so I don't know if they have many heart attacks. As for the risk of a dead bird falling out of the sky and hitting you on the head, I'm guessing the chances are slim. Try not to worry about it.

This Isn't Just Another Fish Story

January 29, 2002

My goldfish swims upside down and looks dead. He has been doing this for a year now and is still eating and pooping. Why does he swim upside down?

Your goldfish swims upside down and looks dead? Big deal. I can do that, although maybe not for a year.

In the course of learning much more about the digestive tracts of goldfish than I ever wanted to know, I came across a piece that said the oldest goldfish on record lived to be 45 years old. I don't know if this is true or not, but you've got to figure that was a long time to be floating around in a goldfish bowl.

Your fish is suffering from air bladder disease, also known as swim bladder disease, and if it has been a year now, you are lucky that it is still alive.

An air bladder is a small sac near the abdomen that fish use to control their buoyancy by diffusing gases from the sac into blood vessels. Goldfish and some other fish also have a pneumocystic duct, something I have no intention of ever spelling again in my life. This duct connects the air bladder to the esophagus so the fish also can adjust its buoyancy by letting air out through its digestive tract.

Fish can get this air bladder ailment from viruses or bacteria, but one of the most common causes is diet, especially food pellets as opposed to food flakes. If the food absorbs too much water when you drop it in the bowl, it will expand in the fish's gut, causing a blockage in that whatchamacallit duct, which causes the fish to lose its balance.

Supposedly you can treat this by wetting the pellets or flakes a bit before you give them to the fish so they have already expanded when the fish eats them.

I am also told giving the fish little bits of frozen peas will solve the problem, although I have no idea why.

I wonder if it has something to do with nitrogen.

Actually, now that I think about, I don't really want to know.

I have other fish to fry.

Small Skulls And Big Eyes, Bob-Bob-Bob

February 19, 2002

Why do birds bob their heads when they walk?

I've got a bad feeling about this one. First of all, it came from a kid, and we all know how devious they can be. It might be a trick question, and every fifth-grader in town will be writing in to tell me how dumb I am. Secondly, this involves pigeons, and whenever I mention pigeons, there's trouble. And it also somehow seems to involve the skull size of extinct archosaurs and that just doesn't sound good at all.

Here goes: Birds have pretty big eyes in relation to the size of their skulls, and to make room for those big eyes, they don't have some muscles that some other creatures do, such as the muscles that move the eye in its socket.

When you walk, your head moves a bit. Those balance-control canals in your ears send a message to your eyeball muscles to move the eye around to compensate for the movement, so your vision isn't like a jerky image from a hand-held camera. Most birds can't do that without moving the whole head.

And to a certain degree, there is the question of where the eyes are. Creatures with front-facing eyes, such as people and owls, can easily draw a bead on something ahead of them. Side-mounted eyes, like pigeons and cows have, give great peripheral vision but limit the field of the straight-ahead binocular vision.

So when a pigeon walks, the head stays back for a beat to get a fix on what it's looking at and then bobs forward again on the next step to take another look. For animals with big heads, the aforementioned cows for example, head-bobbing wouldn't make much sense so they've made other arrangements, like being able to move their eyes in the sockets.

So, anyway, between the need to keep the eyes steady and to keep things in focus, pigeons and some others birds need to go bob-bob-bobbing along.

Where do the extinct archosaurs fit into this? I don't know. I didn't get to that part.

Plucking The Heart Strings Of Bananas
February 27, 2002

What are those bitter-tasting strings of fiber in a banana called, and what is their purpose? The produce man at the grocery store doesn't know. I tried to research this on the computer, but all I got back was a whole bunch of sex sites.

I'm wondering what key words you were using when you were doing the computer search. The mind boggles.

Those strings are called phloem, pronounced "flo-em," with the accent on the first syllable.

It comes from the Greek word *phloos*, meaning bark, as in the bark of a tree.

Sometimes I just can't get over how smart I am.

Bananas are monocots, as are grasses and orchids, palms and other stuff. That's the opposite of dicots, oaks and tomatoes and cotton and the like.

In monocots, the plant's vascular bundles are randomly arranged. In dicots, they are arranged in a circle, which is why you can count the growth rings in an oak.

Which brings us to the heart of the matter: vascular bundles.

Vascular bundles carry water, minerals and foods throughout a plant from the roots to the tippy-tip-tips of the leaves. There are two types, xylem and phloem.

A neutron walks into a bar, orders a drink and asks, "How much?" The bartender says, "For you, no charge."

I just thought I'd drop that in because this whole monocot-dicot-xylem-phloem thing is getting kind of boring, don't you think?

The xylem is kind of woody and delivers water and mineral salts around the plant and also helps hold up the squishy parts.

The phloem delivers sugars and foods from the place in the plant where they are produced to the places in the plant where they are needed.

So, anyway, in answer to the original question, those stringy things are phloem. You can get back to your computer searching now.

Taming Lions And Dodging Church Duty

May 29, 2002

So, I made the mistake Sunday morning of coming into the office just to do one little thing and then I compounded the mistake by stopping to read the mail and listen to my messages, which included today's question.

And so then I started thinking about today's question and pondering it and considering it and generally ruminating upon it and decided I'd just take a quick stab at finding the answer and ended up being half an hour late to church and had to sit way in the back, which really isn't so bad because when you sit way in the back you can visit with your neighbor and also there are fewer people to notice that you were pretending to be tying your shoe when the collection plate went past.

This is the question:

In the old movies and the circus the lion tamer always carried a whip and a gun and a chair. Why a chair?

The answer came from a documentary that came out a few years ago and that I'd forgotten about or at least about the lion-tamer part. It was called *Fast, Cheap & Out of Control* and was very good except for the part about the naked mole rats, which really creeped me out.

The movie included an interview with Dave Hoover, who was a newspaper executive in Ohio before he decided to become a famous lion tamer. In the movie, Hoover says this:

"Lions are very single-minded. When you point the four legs of a chair at them, they get confused. They don't know where to look, and they lose their train of thought."

This sounds reasonable, especially if the lion's train of thought was about to pull into the eat-the-lion-tamer station.

I could try the chair thing on my masters, but I don't think I need to. Little bells and shiny beads are usually enough to distract them.

I did test it out on my cat, but it just gave me one of those looks they give you and walked off.

Maybe I'll try it on Sunday on the guy with the collection plate.

Cats Purr Alone, But Why, How?
June 11, 2002

Do cats purr when there is no one around to hear them?

This is reminiscent of that classic conundrum: If one of my masters says something in an empty conference room and there is no one around to hear what is said, is it still inane?

And the answer to both questions is, well, yes, of course.

While it is true that there are few things more pleasurable than stroking a purring cat, the fact of the matter is the cat is purring for its own benefit and not just to make you all warm and cuddly feeling. Now that I think about it, try to remember the last time a cat did anything for your benefit and not its own.

Cats purr in all manner of situations whether you are around to hear it or not.

Newborns purr when they nurse. Mother cats purr when they are giving birth. Scared or sick or injured cats purr, perhaps as a way of asking for help. Even dying cats have been known to purr.

The thing of it is that no one knows quite for sure why cats purr. Most of us think it's a sign of contentment, but scientists think it may also be a way of communicating with other cats or even a form of comforting themselves, sort of like talking to themselves.

Scientists don't even agree on how cats purr. The most popular theory is that the cat interrupts the flow of air in its larynx and the rising or falling pressure causes its vocal cords to hum. Hence, the purring noise.

Other people think it has something to do with flow of blood to the soft palate at the back of the mouth.

In the course of studying this matter, I found a couple of sources that said wild cats — lions and tigers and jaguars and so forth — do not or cannot purr, but that raccoons can and do.

I do not know for sure if this is true, either the part about the big cats or the part about the raccoon. However, a purring raccoon is not a thought I care to dwell on.

Woe To Fish Within Reach Of Osprey

August 13, 2002

I was fishing on Big Lake recently and enjoyed watching the ospreys fish. I noticed that when they carry the fish they catch, the fish is in line with the bird's body. How do they get them turned to be in line with their bodies without losing hold of the fish?

I am answering this lady's question even though she went on to say I am a "font of useless knowledge." I don't know how I feel about that.

I think I would have preferred "connoisseur" to "font."

This turned out to be pretty interesting or at least I thought so.

An osprey is the only raptor that routinely dives into the water to grab fish. Eagles and others grab them near the surface.

When an osprey sees a fish, it will seem to hover above it briefly and then dive straight down toward it. It hits the water with its talons thrust forward and often ends up all the way under. But it still emerges with a fish and gets airborne again. This is a pretty good trick for a bird that can have a wingspan of up to 6 feet.

At the moment the osprey breaks the water, it adjusts its grip on the fish so the prey's head is pointing forward, which of course gives the bird and its load good aerodynamics.

A bald eagle, on the other hand, will just fly off holding the fish broadside to the wind.

Maybe that's because an eagle is a stronger flier than an osprey and can just muscle its way along. I don't know.

Anyway, ospreys are able to do this deft footwork of rearranging a wriggling fish because their feet and talons are different than an eagle's.

Both birds have three front talons and one back talon on each foot. However, one of the osprey's front talons is opposable, like your thumb, and it can rotate backward.

When an eagle carries away a fish, it has the front toes from both feet on one side of the fish and just the back toes on the other side, which gives the fish at least a chance of thrashing out of the bird's grip.

Ospreys carry their catch with two toes from each foot on either side of the fish.

This means that sucker's pretty well nailed.

So What's A Dog Or Cat Year To Us?
August 22, 2002

Everyone always says one dog year is the equivalent of seven human years, but what about cats? How old is a 1-year-old cat in human years?

I heard a pretty good funny story the other day about how God invented dogs and cats. It was too long to use here, but the punch line was "And so God was happy, and Adam and Eve were happy, and the dog was happy. The cat didn't give a damn one way or the other."

But that doesn't answer the question, does it?

First of all, the thing about dogs turns out to be not quite true. It isn't a straight 1-to-7 thing. For a dog, the first six months is the equivalent of 10 human years. Twelve dog months are 15 of our years. Two dog years, 24 people years. Ten dog years, 56 of ours. A dog would have to be around 15 months old to vote.

I found the dog stuff at www.whisperingstone.com.

As for cats, things are a little murky. I found several sources about this one on the Web, but none of them seem to agree with any of the others. I also found several "cat-years calculators," which were cool, but they didn't seem to agree, either.

Here's one of them anyway, if you want to try it out: www.juliagreen.com.

Don't ask me who Julia Green is. I don't know.

You may, however, ask me about the oldest known cat on record. It was some cat in England that lived to be 34 and died in 1957. I'm sure it was a nice animal, but you have to admit 34 years is a long time to have the same cat hanging around.

Here's one rule of thumb for figuring out your cat's age in human years: The first six cat months equal 13 human years. The second six months equals eight years, which makes the cat 21 in human years. The second cat year is 10 human years and each subsequent year is three human years. So five cat years would be 40 human years. President Bush, by the way, is 10 in cat years.

So anyway, punch up one of those cat-age calculators and figure out how old the beast is in human years. Then you can share that with your cat, not that it'll give a damn one way or another.

Cottontails Have One Mean Kick
September 19, 2002

I have here a letter from a guy in Scottsdale who is having a debate with his son-in-law over reality. The son-in-law says reality is what we perceive it to be. The father-in-law says reality exists apart from our perceptions. They want me to settle it.

People, people, people. This newspaper only costs 50 cents. For 50 cents you do not get thoughtful discussions on the nature of reality. For 50 cents you get questions such as this:

Why do rabbits have white tails? They really blend into the background until they run and then you see their white tails like a target.

There is a school of thought that holds that the cottontail's white tail is a deliberate giveaway, that without it the animal would be so well-camouflaged that its predators couldn't find it at all, and rabbits would take over the world. That doesn't sound quite right to me.

A rabbit's tail, by the way, is called a scut. It comes from a Middle English word meaning rabbit or hare. Here's another good rabbit word, fomm. A fomm is a little pocket shelter a rabbit makes by trampling down grass or small shrubs. I don't know where the word comes from, but if you got it on a triple-word square you'd get 33 points in Scrabble.

Anyway, if you looked at the tail of a desert cottontail, you would see the fur is darker on the top and white underneath.

When a rabbit is frightened, it takes off running in a zigzag pattern and flashes the white underside of the tail as an alarm signal to other rabbits.

Sometimes during the chase, the rabbit will stop suddenly and freeze, sitting on the white part of the tail. The idea, I guess, is to confuse its pursuer.

All of this can't be all that effective because snakes, coyotes, hawks and other predators eat rabbits like popcorn. Something like 80 percent of rabbits don't make it through their first year.

We think of rabbits as timid, but they can daze a small predator by thumping them with their back legs, which, if you think about, has to be pretty embarrassing from the small predator's point of view.

Lessons In French, Navigation
January 14, 2003

I just read a story that said the average workweek in France is 29.5 hours, one of the lowest among developed nations. And many French workers complain about their long hours.

Cela n'est pas grand? Est merveilleux. This, of course, has nothing to do with today's topic. I just thought I'd mention it. We could learn a lot from the French. Now, the question:

What is the controlling force that directs the turns of a flock of pigeons? They all seem to make a turn at the same time without any going astray. Is there a drill sergeant in the flock?

That sort of synchronized turning of a flock of pigeons or any other birds is called flocking, and it is common not only to birds but to schools of fish and some other animals. I'm not sure that anyone knows exactly how it works — *les oiseau; comment myserious!* — but there are some ideas floating around.

For starters, flocks of birds do not have leaders as such. At any given moment, any old bird might be out in front.

This is probably a good thing for us. It's kind of like my masters; if they ever got organized, they could be really dangerous. Can you imagine what might happen if some rogue bird declared itself King of the Pigeons and brought other pigeons into a coordinated force? *Une idee effrayante, mon amis.*

Several years ago, a scientist named Kenneth Able filmed flocks of sandpipers and then analyzed the film at very slow speeds. He discovered that the flock seems to always follow the lead of a bird that is banking toward the flock, which mostly helps the group react rapidly to attacks by predators and helps prevent indecision.

What was so incredible about this is how quickly the flock reacts.

Able found that the birds immediately adjacent to the initiator took about 67 milliseconds to adjust their courses. However, it then took just 15 milliseconds for a change in course to pass from bird to bird like a wave through the flock.

Apparently birds that are on the far side of the flock from the individual that instigated the turn are able to estimate or anticipate the arrival of the maneuver. It's kind of like people in a stadium who see the Wave coming and stand up and flap their arms around at the right time.

Note: It has come to my attention that the other day some idiot using my name identified the late Byrd Howell Granger, the noted expert on Arizona place names, as a male. She wasn't.

Je suis desole.

And now, what's 29.5 divided by 5? Whoa, time to go home.

Itching To Study Chiggers?
August 14, 2003

I can't figure out the life cycle of chiggers. They burrow under your skin and irritate you for a week and that's it? Why don't they become extinct?

Gee, I wish you hadn't asked that. Just thinking about chiggers makes me all itchy. Aside from my masters, I can't think of anything much more annoying than chiggers. And driving in Tucson. That too. It's a perfectly nice town, but for some reason driving in Tucson just drives me crazy.

Oh, and Céline Dion. She's annoying too.

Fortunately, we are not much troubled by chiggers here in the Valley. They are not creatures of the desert. This is not to say you will never get a chigger bite here, but you are much more likely to be afflicted if you are hiking or camping or generally messing around in other parts of the state.

About the only good thing I can think of about chiggers is they do not spread infectious diseases. You have to give them credit for that.

The chigger that makes you itchy is actually the larval stage of the chigger mite. The mite's life cycle has seven stages. If you ask me, that seems like a lot of stages just to produce some crummy mite, but there you have it. The stages are egg, deutovum, larva, protonymph, deuto-nymph, tritonymph and adult. Don't ask me what most of them mean. I don't know. I'm not even sure some of them are spelled right.

As I said, it's the larvae that you need to worry about. Nymphs and adults mostly prey on insects.

Anyway, the reader's premise is faulty. Chiggers don't burrow under your skin. And, unlike my masters, they do not suck blood. What a chigger usually does is attach itself to the base of a hair follicle and inject you with chigger spit that contains enzymes that break down skin cells. Then they suck up your liquefied skin.

Euuuuu.

You don't even know this is happening at first because the itching doesn't start for a few hours, and, besides, a chigger is about 1/120th of an inch long, so it's not like you're going to see it at work.

So the chigger sucks away at you for three or four days until it is engorged and then drops off and goes about its business. In the course of researching this question, I came across a picture of an engorged chigger, and, trust me, you should be glad they don't run pictures in this column. It's not the sort of thing you want to see at breakfast.

Chiggers mostly live about 50 to 70 days, but females can live up to a year, wintering in the soil and cranking out more chiggers in the spring.

Chigger spit. Euuu.

Repeat After Me: M.Y.O.D.B.
August 30, 2003

So, this 10-year-old boy is sitting on a park bench smoking a big cigar and eating one candy bar after another. A lady walks by and watches him for a while and then says, "Little boy, it can't be healthy for you to be smoking a cigar and eating all that candy."

The boy says, "My grandfather lived to be 102."

The lady says, "And did he smoke cigars and eat so much candy?"

The kid says, "No, he minded his own damn business."

That's not much of a joke, I suppose. It's not nearly as funny as the talking parrot joke. However, I use it here to illustrate my new philosophy for solving, if not all, at least some of the world's problems:

"Let's just all mind our own damn business."

Obviously, this cannot apply in every situation, but just think how much social, religious, cultural, sexual or even political strife we could be spared if we all just butted out. And there would be more time for pie.

And here's the corollary to my new philosophy: Try not to get your name in the newspaper. Sure, sometimes getting your name in the paper might be a good thing, if it's for getting a medal or something. However, for the most part, people get their names in the newspaper for being stupid. Or evil. Or dead.

So the next time you're faced with some tough decision, my advice is to ask yourself: A) Is this my business? B) Do I want to get my name in the newspaper because of this?

And C) I wonder if there's any pie left?

Sorry, I'm just a bit cranky today. Let's move on to something more productive.

I'm a vegetarian. Can I put my dog and two cats on a vegetarian diet? I don't feel right about feeding them meat when I won't eat it.

According to the Pet Food Manufacturers Association, it is possible to feed a dog a balanced vegetarian diet.

Cats, however, are what you call "obligate carnivores," which means, according to the pet food people, they need meat.

Specifically, old Puff needs an amino acid called taurine, which is found almost exclusively in meat.

Taurine is necessary in cats for good eyesight, good reproductive and cardiac health and some other stuff, including "bile formation." Like cats need more bile.

Cats apparently can manufacture a bit of taurine on their own. Maybe that's what they're doing when they look that way cats look sometimes. But they also need a supplementary source.

Anyway, before you start messing around with your pets' diets, maybe you should check with your vet.

Not that it's any of my business.

Stay Calm In That Snake Pit
December 18, 2003

I was thinking of saving today's question until next spring when the rattlesnakes come out of hibernation, but apparently there is some kind of argument involved so I am going to deal with it now before tension between the two sides escalates and things get out of hand.

Also, I thought if I held it for a while I could use the time to practice spelling "ovoviviparous."

You people shouldn't argue so much, especially at Christmastime. You should try to be sweet and agreeable and tolerant. Like me.

Here's the question:

Could you settle an argument that we are having at our club? Some say that rattlesnakes are born live. Others say they are hatched from eggs. Also, what do they feed on until they are large enough to forage on their own?

Ovoviviparous is a pretty good word. I wonder how many other words there are with three v's in them. I'll probably be sorry I wondered about that.

Rattlesnakes are ovoviviparous. So are some other reptiles, fish and snails. Ovoviviparous means the little baby snakes develop in eggs, but they hatch out of the eggs inside the mother and are born live. So both sides are right in this case.

As for eating, baby rattlesnakes are pretty much on their own right from the start. In some species, the rattlesnake mom will leave a scent trail so the babies can find their way back to the den for the first week or so, but the young ones have to find their own eats.

Baby rattlesnakes can be nasty little things. They are born with venom and are perfectly willing to use it. The problem is that when an adult rattlesnake bites you, it may or may not inject you with venom. With baby rattlesnakes, it's all venom all the time. They don't hold back.

On the other hand, the survival rate is not great. Many snakes don't make it through their first year, although if they do and their luck continues, they can live as long as 25 years.

As long as we're on the subject, did you know a female rattlesnake may go for months without eating in the year she is going to give birth? That's one reason females don't reproduce until they are about 7 or so years old and why they only give birth every two or three years. It takes a lot out of them.

Here's another thing about rattlesnake reproduction. The actual fertilization of the eggs usually doesn't take place until a long time after the mating. The female stores the sperm in a chamber called the cloaca until she's good and ready to use it, usually about five or so months later.

Try A Little Hair Of The (Wet) Dog
February 26, 2004

Today, class, we are going to don our frilly white aprons, rubber gloves and hip waders and discuss good housekeeping. To wit:

The other day I gave my dog a bath, and he was nice and clean and smelled good and then he went out in the rain and now the whole house smells like wet dog. How can I get rid of the smell?

For starters, you could either sell the dog or the house, but I suppose you're going to want to quibble about that, so we'll have to go to Plan B.

Of course, part of the reason the dog came back in smelling bad is that dogs don't like smelling clean. That's why they roll around in poop or dead things or smelly wet grass — they think it masks their dog smell from their prey, even if their prey is just a bowl of Alpo.

Now you could just go to the grocery store or a pet store and find all sorts of deodorizers or cleaners or whatever that would do the job, but I suppose that would just be too easy for you people. You're looking for a challenge.

As for the dog, I'm told that you can wipe the beast down with sheets of fabric softener. I don't know about that. Fabric softener makes me itch, so I'm not sure what it might do to a dog. Just put the animal outside until it smells better.

As for your house, why don't you just give the place a good cleaning? It could probably use it anyway. Sprinkle baking soda on the carpets or rugs and let it sink in a bit before you vacuum. That would be good for starters.

I read one homemaking tip from a woman who operates a wig store. She recommended mixing water and vodka in a one-to-one ratio and spraying it on stuff, like the chair on which the wet dog curled up or on the dog's bed or things like that. Apparently this eliminates odors and evaporates quickly and won't make your house smell like a still.

If that seems like a waste of good vodka to you, try this: Mix two cups of fabric softener and two cups of baking soda into four cups of warm water. Then spritz it around on stuff.

Or if you really like spritzing — and who doesn't? — try one quart of hydrogen peroxide with one-quarter cup of baking soda and one teaspoon of dish soap.

Mowing Down Seeds Of Doubt
March 17, 2004

The other night while mowing my father's front yard, as I have done for nearly 30 years, I wondered if it is the same Bermuda grass that I cut when I started doing this to earn my allowance, many, many, many years ago.

Thirty years? Wow. I hope this guy's father has been increasing his allowance over all that time.

Anyway, did you know you can make flour out of Bermuda grass? It doesn't sound like an especially good idea to me, but apparently it can be done. I know this from reading a proposal for a study "to investigate the human nutritional adequacy of Bermuda grass flours from experimental and standard Bermuda grasses: World Feeder, Gordon's Gift, and Tifton."

This was a project of the Oklahoma Center for the Advancement of Science and Technology, which I am guessing is some place in Oklahoma. I couldn't find out how the study came out, and what with all those fertilizers and weed killers and stuff people put on their lawns, I wouldn't be baking up any Bermuda grass muffins if I were you.

Nice, clean, unpolluted Bermuda grass also is supposed to be very good for chinchillas, if you happen to have any chinchillas around the house.

OK, enough stalling: Has this guy been mowing the same grass all this time?

Well, yeah, I guess so. Or at least he has been mowing the descendants of the same Bermuda grass for 30 years.

Bermuda grass, as you probably know if you've ever tried to get rid of it, is pretty tough stuff. It loves bright sun, it can take a lot of heat and it's fairly drought resistant.

Bermuda grass is stoloniferous, a word I only use to show off. It means it has stolons, which are surface roots that travel along above ground and root at their joints, growing new plants. So if your lawn is made up of Bermuda grass, you have stolon property. Get it? Stolon. Stolen. That was a good one.

So anyway, those stolons are running around all over your yard putting down roots, which sprout new grass, which in turn sends out more stolons. Bermuda grass, of course, also produces seeds, especially if stressed by drought, and the seeds produce more roots and stolons and so on and so forth.

When it turns cold, the whole mess goes dormant and bides its time until the warm weather returns, and then it starts up all over again.

So, yes, I guess this guy has been mowing the same family of grass for 30 years. Somehow that sounds kind of depressing to me, but if he doesn't mind and the chinchillas are happy, I guess I shouldn't worry about it.

Rainy Days And Phoenix: A Great Combo

April 9, 2004

Why is it that every time I visit Phoenix from my home in Michigan it rains?

I have no idea. I suspect it is a mere coincidence, but I think you should visit more often. We could use the rain.

Well, that didn't take long. Let's do another one.

I have heard the daddy longlegs is the most poisonous spider in the country, but its jaws are too weak to penetrate human skin. Is that true?

Huh? The daddy longlegs? Are we talking about the same spider? The one with the long, skinny legs and the little body? Poisonous?

Heavenly days, I just don't know who puts ideas like this in the heads of you people. Sometimes I think that if it weren't for this column and *Insects of the Southwest* by Floyd Werner and good old Carl Olson, some of you people would get so bad off that finally you'd just forget to breathe.

Daddy longlegs aren't even really spiders. They're related to spiders, scorpions and ticks, but they aren't really spiders. Spiders have fangs. Daddy longlegs don't have fangs. Spiders are venomous to one degree or another. Daddy longlegs are not venomous.

So let's review: A) Not really a spider. B) No fangs. C) No venom. All these things very much work against the idea that the daddy longlegs is the most venomous spider in the country.

You people.

Daddy longlegs like dark, damp places or a nice, lush garden. They mostly eat insects and the like, and they defend themselves by throwing off some awful-smelling secretion. And if one of those long legs gets caught in a spider web, a daddy longlegs just snaps it off and goes on about its business.

All this does raise the question of exactly which spider around here is the most venomous. Beats me. I suppose it's either the black widow or the Arizona brown spider.

Neither one of them is likely to kill you, but the bite of a brown spider can be very nasty indeed.

The area of the bite starts to ache, you feel kind of like you have the flu, and then a blister forms around the bite and the skin eventually turns black and falls off. Yuck.

Arizona brown spiders are related to the recluse spider of the Midwest. The way to tell them apart is that Arizona browns have three pairs of eyes and recluses have four.

I personally have never counted spider eyes, but if you want to, be my guest.

Life in Arizona, such as it is...

OK, so remember in that last section when I said that part, the part about plants and animals and so forth, was my favorite part of this book? Well, it was OK, I guess, but now I've decided this part, the Arizona part, is my favorite.

Such a place to live in. One day mountain lions are chasing people around in Tucson and the next day trout are rising up on a cold stream just an easy drive away from the Valley and the day after that you find your flip-flops have melted into the asphalt in Phoenix. And then there's quicksand. At least it's not boring.

Having said all that, I hasten to add that if you don't live here now, you shouldn't move here. We have quite enough people as it is and some of them are kind of annoying. Like those people who talk on their cell phones through those headsets. You're standing there in line next to them and all of the sudden they start blurting out stuff like they had that Tourette's Syndrome thing or something. After a bit, you figure out that they are having a phone conversation in public. Like I want to hear all this? Shaa.

And besides, you can always watch Arizona travel documentaries on public television or wherever and get the same effect without all the trouble of sorting out all that stuff in your garage and moving here yourself. If you really want to move, I hear that Oregon is very nice. Maybe you should move to Oregon. But unless you're prepared to live under brutal desert conditions and live with a drought and the monsoon and Gila monsters and their ilk and with a bunch of people who moved here because they didn't fit in anywhere normal, I don't think you should move here. Unless, of course, you're prepared to offer me an obscenely high price for my house, in which case I guess you'd fit in here just fine.

It's not like I'm a native myself, although I have been here a good long while. You know how it is: You're young and you move for an adventure, and you figure you'll just stay a couple years and then move back to some place where you would actually want to raise a family and where it might actually rain. Before you know it the kids are in school and the credit-card people have got a pretty good lock on where you are and it doesn't look like you'll give them the slip again anyway. By now a couple of governors have been indicted and the girl at the dry cleaners, the one with that tattoo, is calling you by name, and you figure, what the heck, you might as well stick around a bit and see what happens next.

And even after all these years, I'm still not sure what will happen next. But if you're not already here, just stay put. If anything really neat happens, I'll let you know. If you are already here, cool. Is this a great place to be or what? Just turn off your cell phone, will you? Or else move back to Ohio. It rains there.

Basements No Bargain In Arizona

May 30, 1999

Q: *My wife says there are no basements here because there are no tornadoes, so we don't need a place to hide. I say it's because the ground is too hard. Who's right?*

A: First of all, your question is flawed by asserting there are no basements around here. Granted, there aren't many, but there are some, especially in older homes. They're relatively plentiful in the Encanto neighborhood of Phoenix and in some scattered pockets of pre-World War II homes around the Valley.

They're not the pine-paneled rumpus-room basements you recall from your split level back in Moline, Ill., but they're basements nonetheless.

And, as we shall see, basements have made somewhat of a comeback in recent years in upper-end new housing.

But the vast majority of Phoenix-area houses are squatting on concrete slabs, meaning that if we ever really did have a tornado, your best bet would be a merciful God.

So, why no subterranean space?

"Because it's cheaper to go up than it is to go down," said Earl Gibbons, a soil specialist for Construction Inspection and Testing Co. in Phoenix.

It isn't that the soil around here is necessarily too hard, Gibbons said. It's just that the soil isn't quite right.

"We have sandy conditions in a lot of areas, and it's hard to excavate sand because it keeps collapsing in," he said.

And if it isn't sand, it's rock or clay, which tends to be very dry, leaving a lot of air pockets and making it hard to backfill.

In colder climes, builders are required to dig deep to get below the frost line. In the Valley, the frost line is something you get on your lip from drinking a Slurpee.

There are less tangible factors involved as well.

Do you have fond childhood memories of carefree hours wiled away playing hide-and-seek in your grandma's basement?

No, you don't, because chances are, Grandma's basement was a dark, damp place with lots of cobwebs and dusty Mason jars full of stewed tomatoes and a rustling sound over in the darkest corner that probably was just mice.

"We've found that basements aren't really a selling feature for most people," said Susan Gaupel, an executive assistant at Continental Homes.

"People come here for the sunshine and don't want to be reminded of the doom and gloom of the Midwest. Basements just kind of remind them of a cold winter."

Or whatever made that rustling sound in the corner.

Still, some people dig basements, and for good reason. Basements provide storage space for unpacked moving boxes and visiting relatives, and they give shelter from the heat.

"At 6 feet down, it is a constant 60 degrees temperature," according to Scott McDonald, owner of The Wall Company in Phoenix. "When you walk into a basement, you really can feel the temperature dropping."

McDonald should know. His company, which he started about seven years ago with his father, exists to dig basements. Gibbons estimated The Wall Company digs 75 percent to 80 percent of the basements that get dug around here.

"That's what we specialize in — basements," McDonald said. "We probably do about 300 a year."

It's not easy and it's not cheap. Because of the above-noted soil conditions, McDonald's crews need heavier equipment than your standard-issue backhoe and often need to add moisture to the soil around basement walls to keep it solid.

All this adds up to about $13 to $17 per square foot of basement and tacks about 30 days on to the building schedule, he said. So most of McDonald's basements are beneath homes in the $200,000-and-up range or tucked under ritzy additions.

In other words, they're not bargain basements.

Roaches, One Of God's Mysteries
August 1, 1999

Q: *We thought we left cockroaches behind in Chicago. Instead, we find they're huge out here. My wife is completely freaked.*

A: Oh, yeah, and you're not freaked?

Perhaps no crawly thing, aside from the Legislature, invokes more horror and disgust than a big old sewer roach skittering around your bathtub or grazing on a box of saltines in the cupboard. Or coming at you across the sheets.

Roaches. We hate 'em. God probably had some good reason when he created them, but it's a mystery to mortals.

Perhaps it was to keep us humble. Scientists have said their survivability is such that, in the event of a nuclear holocaust, roaches would dominate the charred new world. This raises an interesting question: If we wiped out our world with nuclear bombs and only roaches survived and evolved, would there be, in a gazillion or so years, a roach Jerry Springer Show?

Anyway, we're infested with three kinds here in the Valley and, reflecting our diversity, they are the German roach, the Turkestan roach and the good old American roach.

The small German model is most likely to take up permanent residence in your house. They like kitchens, especially the insides of electrical appliances. They can fly but prefer to scurry.

The big ugly suckers you're seeing are the Turkestan and the American. They're gross and are lumped together under the term "sewer roach," but only the American is usually found in sewers.

It can be hard to tell an American from the Turkestan if you already whomped it with a Size 12 Florsheim.

However, in its pre-whomped state, the Turkestan roach is about an inch long, brown to black, and it actually prefers the out-of-doors. If it is inside, like any roach, it's going to want a drink and will likely end up in or near a sink or tub.

The American roach runs up to about 2 inches, is shiny and brown and sometimes flies. Ayaaaaaa!

The American roach, according to *Insects of the Southwest*, by Floyd Werner and Carl Olson, was once nominated as the official U.S.

insect but was rejected by the Entomological Society of the United States in favor of the monarch butterfly.

Just think, if roaches had become the official national bug, they might have become a flash point for protesters, and we might now be debating a constitutional amendment to outlaw the burning of an American roach or whomping it with footwear.

Yes, the American roach dwells in sewers. (A city employee once told us it looks like the walls are moving. Euuuu!) Contrary to what some think, however, they don't swim up the pipes into your home.

It is theoretically possible, because roaches can swim (and survive on wallpaper glue and, in some countries, vote). But roaches are most likely to enter your house through openings around pipes or wires, under loose weather-stripping, through pet doors, or any other opening that presents itself.

We say hanging's too good for them, plus they reproduce faster than you can tie the nooses. The Florsheim approach can be viscerally satisfying, but you have to find them before you can whomp them. Roaches are nocturnal, so the best hunting is at night.

We once read that if you spray roaches with dish detergent, it eats away at some sort of protective outer skeleton and leaves the roach to die a lingering, awful death. It's a nice thought, but chasing a roach with a bottle of Palmolive is time-consuming, messy and undignified.

Geckos, those little lizards you see on fences and outside walls, are said to be hell on roaches. But trading bugs for lizards isn't everybody's idea of victory.

Cleanliness is next to roachlessness. Keep your cupboards and countertops free of crumbs, keep food containers sealed shut. Don't leave pet food out in the open unnecessarily. You know what they feed roaches in research facilities? Dry dog food.

Plug up any openings around pipes or wires, inside and outside.

Most Valley cities will dispatch a crew to dust manhole covers in your neighborhood for roaches. Look in your city's listings in the Blue Pages, usually under the sewer department.

Boric acid is a good deterrent, but if you're going the do-it-your-self extermination route, be sure to read all the warnings on the label. Your best bet is probably regular visits by a good exterminator.

Roaches — spray 'em, gas 'em, starve 'em, whomp 'em. Show no mercy. In a gazillion years, they'd do the same to you.

Religion, Sex And Winter Lawns
October 10, 1999

Q: *I just survived my first Arizona summer, and the worst part was mowing my lawn in the triple-digit heat. Now, my neighbor asked me if I am going to put in a winter lawn. Am I?*

A: First of all, congratulations on your getting through your first summer. You are now officially qualified to lord it over other newcomers and to say of future summers, "Of course, this is nothing like the summer of '99."

And you may now truly appreciate the sweet fruit of a Valley winter, although it isn't really so much winter as it is not-summer.

As to the winter lawn, there are two schools of thought.

School One: It looks good, it's worth the effort and if all your neighbors put in a winter lawn and you don't, it will look bad and the whole neighborhood will slide into decay, and by spring it will just be a row of crack houses and sharecroppers' hovels.

School Two: Bag that. You spent the past seven or eight months risking heatstroke to mow the lawn, and now the damn thing is dying off for the winter like it's supposed to. Good riddance. Grass isn't supposed to grow in the desert, anyway.

School One: "Slob."

School Two: "Neat freak."

School One: "And if I catch your bratty kids picking my grapefruit and throwing them at the mailbox again, I'm calling the cops."

School Two: "Oh yeah. Well, if I catch your mangy dog in my flower bed again, I'll take him to the pound."

So, as we can see, winter lawns, like religion and certain sexual practices, are a deeply personal decision best left to the individual conscience.

If you do decide to put in a winter lawn — and we're not saying you should or shouldn't — here are a few tips.

First of all, don't jump the gun. If you start your winter lawn when it's still too hot — nighttime temperatures should be in the mid-60s — you'll end up having to do it twice.

Buy the best seed you can afford. Annual ryegrass is popular because it's cheap. Perennial rye seed costs a little more, but most people agree it looks better.

Scatter the seed. This will make you very popular with all the birds in the neighborhood.

Then cover it lightly with forest mulch or steer or horse manure. Manure will of course stink up the whole neighborhood for a while, but it is very effective and is in plentiful supply, even when the Legislature is not in session.

Watering is very important. Water gently to avoid scattering the seeds, and water frequently. For the first 10 days or so, you should sprinkle the new seeds at least three times a day, tapering off as the new lawn establishes itself.

When your winter lawn is ready for the first mowing, feed it with a nitrogen-based fertilizer.

Then drive around the neighborhood looking at other people's lawns and comparing them with your own. A colleague of ours described this as "an alpha-male thing."

On the other hand, you can park yourself in a comfy chair, tune the radio to the game, crack a cold one and watch your neighbor do all the work while your lawn dies a quiet and well-deserved death.

Take your pick.

Wallace And Ladmo, Gone But Not Forgotten

October 17, 1999

Q: *My husband and I moved here almost a year ago. We were at a dinner not long ago with three other couples and everyone except us was talking about Wallace and Ladmo? Who are they?*

A: Alas, dear lady, it is not who they are, it is who they were.

And, alas again, you may live here the rest of your life, you may wear bola ties and turquoise jewelry and string Christmas lights on a cactus and be elected governor and then get indicted, but you will never be a true resident of the Valley if you did not grow up, in some way, with Wallace and Ladmo.

On the other hand, any Valley child of that era could today walk into a room full of strangers anywhere in the world and say, "Ho, ho, ha, ha, hee, hee, ho, ho," and if there is another Valley expatriate present, he will have found a friend in a faraway place.

Wallace and Ladmo, in its simplest definition, was a children's show that ran on Channel 5 (KPHO), then an independent station, from 1954 to 1989. It started in an era when almost every station had its own weekday kids program — any Duane and Floppy alums out there? — and featured a live studio audience, skits and cartoons.

The show starred Bill Thompson as Wallace and the late Ladimir Kwiatkowski as Ladmo. Over the years it featured a number of other performers, most notably Pat McMahon, of KTAR fame, who starred as Captain Super, Aunt Maud, that rotten little kid Gerald and other characters.

But calling Wallace and Ladmo a children's show is a bit like calling pâté de foie gras a nice dip. It was a children's show that sported an attitude. A sponsor's ice cream was once described on air by our heroes as "Good. Not great, but good." Sponsors clamored to buy airtime in hopes of being so abused.

Republic reporter and longtime TV writer Dave Walker spent his Wonder Bread years watching Wall-boy and Lad.

"Aside from dispensing cartoons and candy, the Wallace and Ladmo troupe was expert at gentle social satire. While adept at broad comedy, the key players had a wicked eye for detail," Walker said.

"Decades later, I finally understood why my parents were laughing, too. The show lampooned little old ladies as the Valley desperately attempted to attract retirees, superheroes at the same time Batman played in prime time, and teen-dream pop groups while pop groups ruled the world."

Richard Ruelas, a *Republic* reporter and author of *Ho Ho! Ha Ha! Hee Hee! Ho Ho! — The Wallace and Ladmo Show: 35 Years of Laughter,* said the show "permanently demented Phoenix children for three generations."

"Wallace was way ahead of his time. His show had a parody of a rock band called Hub Kapp and the Wheels 30 years before Spinal Tap. He had on a clown who hated kids 20 years before David Letterman had Flunky the Late Night Clown.

"When people from other cities ask me about Wallace and Ladmo, I try to tell them it was like Captain Kangaroo or Bozo the Clown, only it was funny. Really funny. So funny you didn't stop watching it after you became a teenager."

A staple of the television show and of the live appearances by Wallace, Ladmo and Gerald was the Ladmo bag — a small paper bag stuffed with the sponsors' goodies and handed out to a few lucky children in the audience. There are among us today grown men and women, responsible and sober people of great accomplishments, who will tell you without hesitation that winning a Ladmo bag was one of the happiest moments of their lives, if not the happiest.

(We personally have a personal daughter who once was personally handed a Ladmo bag by Ladmo himself while Gerald — oooo, he was a rotten kid — loudly suggested that she keep it out of the reach of her big fat father.)

When the show ended in 1989 with Thompson's retirement, the Valley was thunderstruck. This is not an exaggeration. When Kwiatkowski died at age 65 in 1994, the Valley mourned. Thompson — who by the way is no relation, but we wish he were — still lives here.

Hail to thee, blithe spirits.

Cactus Cups Cut Cold
December 14, 1999

Q: *My husband and I recently drove to Cave Creek and along the way we noticed many people had put plastic-foam cups on their cactuses. I said this is for protection from the frost, but my husband said it was some sort of Christmas decoration. Who wins?*

A: You know, your mother was right: You could have done better.

As entertaining as it would be to tell you that, yes, placing plastic-foam cups on cactuses is a treasured holiday tradition dating back to the earliest Spanish settlers, we must tell the truth: Your husband is 100 percent wrong.

The cups are for frost protection.

We doubled-checked this with Patrick Quirk, a cactus horticulturist at the Desert Botanical Garden, which, by the way, is a swell place and a great spot to dump winter visitors for an afternoon.

Plastic-foam cups can trap just enough warmer air to protect the growing tip of a cactus. Plus, they won't blow off, and they're easier to use than the old sheet or whatever that you might use to cover your petunias on a chilly night.

And we have more chilly nights than you might expect. The dates of the first and last frosts vary depending on what part of the Valley you live in. Generally, the outlying parts of town are chillier than the closer-in neighborhoods. For instance, the average first and last frost dates for Laveen are Nov. 27 and Feb. 21, while the average season at Sky Harbor International Airport is Dec. 12 to Feb. 7.

Cactuses seem to have survived around here for ages without the benefit of foam cups. So why start now?

Because, Quirk said, the becupped cactuses you saw probably weren't from around here.

Cactuses have adapted to cold weather as far north as Cape Cod, and our local varieties, such as the saguaro, aren't especially at risk from frost.

But homeowners or landscapers who bring in cactus from farther south — Mexico or the Caribbean or South America — need to take steps to protect their imports.

Why Build Up When You Can Sprawl Out?
February 13, 2000

Q: *Why are there no tall buildings around here?*

A: No tall bildins? Golleee, mister, why this here newspaper bildin its own self is 10 whole stories tall. Why, that's taller than two silos!

Sorry, we couldn't resist slipping into our world-famous Gomer Pyle imitation.

Why are there no tall buildings around here?

That's a good question and to get a good answer we went straight to good old Max Underwood, a professor of architecture at Arizona State University and an expert in Phoenix architecture who has on more than one occasion made us sound smart.

"One reason is that there is so much space available that they didn't need to build tall buildings," Underwood said. "It's a lot more expensive to build up than out."

On the other hand, Chicago, for example, is penned in by Lake Michigan, so if you want big, the only way to go is up.

Another reason, he said, is that Arizona developed later than big cities whose skylines took their shapes during the Age of Skyscrapers.

One more reason — boy, is Underwood smart or what? — businesses are changing. Many corporations are leaner (and often meaner) than they used to be, and they don't need to pack so many workers into a centralized space. And modern communications, especially computers, mean workforces can be decentralized.

And communications and media mean that corporations such as Sears, as in the Sears Tower in Chicago, or Transamerica, as in the Transamerica Building in San Francisco, don't need gigantic skyscrapers to establish their identity in the public mind.

For the record, the tallest building in Arizona is the Bank One Building in downtown Phoenix — 40 floors, 570 feet.

Back in 1986, we were all mesmerized by a French businessman named Georges Schriqui, who came to town and announced he was going to build the world's tallest building right here in Phoenix, although why he wanted to do this we can't seem to recall. It was going to be 114 stories tall and cost $800 million.

As it turned out, nobody actually had $800 million, or at least not $800 million to spend building the world's tallest building.

Schriqui said a big French financial institution had agreed to finance the project, but after talks with Schriqui, a spokesman for the institution said, "C'est a point mort," which is French for "That dog don't hunt."

Beware The Slimy Parasite
April 17, 2001

Today's question:

We were hiking near Lake Mohave recently, and we saw plants covered with an orange stringy substance that looked like "silly string." It had little teeth. What was it?

Just as a measure of my self-restraint I am going to answer your question about a slimy, creepy parasite with little teeth that sucks the life out of other plants without making a single reference to my masters. I think this shows great discipline and self-control, don't you?

What you saw is a slimy, creepy parasitic plant commonly called dodder. It once was thought to be related to morning glories, but now it is classified in the genus *Cuscuta*, which is certainly more than I wanted to know about it, but there you have it.

It is a stringy yellow or orange plant that twines itself around other plants. It can be very destructive to crops and ornamentals alike. Its victims include alfalfa, clover potatoes, chrysanthemums, dahlias, ivy and petunias.

Dodder does contain some chlorophyll so it can make its own food, but it gets most of its nutrition by sucking water, minerals and carbohydrates from its host. It, of course, does not really have teeth. A plant with teeth would be really creepy. It does have a kind of modified root system called haustoria that it uses to suck the host plant dry. I don't think that for what I get paid I should have to spell chrysanthemums and haustoria in the same story, but the effort involved keeps my mind from straying from my intent not to mention my masters.

In addition to being a parasite, it also spreads disease. I would list some of the diseases, but many of them are hard to spell. My favorite one on the list was "pear decline," which is a name I like a lot for a disease. As in: "My doctors says I have pear decline. Cough, cough. I think I got it from my masters."

Mockingbird Busy Singing Love Songs

May 8, 2001

Today's question:

Lately some bird has been singing in our yard late at night. It's loud enough to keep us awake. Are there nightingales around here?

We'll get to this is a minute, but first: A number of you have called or written about last week's Big Dipper question. Yes, I know perfectly well that it is the Earth's spin that gives the illusion the stars are rotating. Thank you. Surely you didn't expect me to cut out cheap shots and bad jokes in order to make room for facts, did you?

And what is it with you people and birds lately? Wouldn't you rather hear about my recent hand-to-scale combat with a snake the size of a sewer pipe? Of course, it turned out to be a plain old non-venomous gopher snake, but it was a crabby non-venomous gopher snake. Really crabby. I suppose you'd be crabby too if I picked you up with a rake and dropped you over a fence. Still it was quite an ordeal for us both, and for a modest fee I could re-enact it at a children's party, wedding reception or bar mitzvah.

OK, as to your bird: No, we do not have nightingales around here. It is a mockingbird that is keeping you awake at night. This is the mating and nesting season for mockingbirds, and your backyard is a great big mockingbird singles bar with the males busy defending their territory and trying to impress babes. This they do by singing loudly, especially on moonlit nights.

And since it is mating and nesting season, this also is the time of year when mockingbirds and some other birds are especially aggressive in defending their turf. This is why some of you have written rather indignantly as of late to complain of being dive-bombed by birds in the sanctity of your own yard. Mockingbirds seem to be especially tough on pets, especially cats, in the defense of their home lands. They are feisty rascals.

Bluster All You Want: This Is Arizona's Big Event
June 20, 2001

When I first came here to toil in the vineyards of *The Phoenix Gazette*, I frequently left the office in the late afternoon or evening in the company of the city editor, the immortal Lois Boyles.

Often in the summer we would go outside to find the evening sky was a sort of sickly pinkish-green, and the air was filled with dirt and grit scoured off the ground by a hot, dry wind. Sometimes, a few drops of rain would fall and trigger that hot-asphalt smell.

"Oh, boy," Lois would say with the delight. "We're having a dust storm. Isn't this great?"

I thought she was hopelessly insane.

Things change.

Maybe if a storm has dropped a tree on your house, you'll feel differently, but as for me, I have come to kind of like, even enjoy, the monsoon.

I like those clouds that pile up as the day progresses, pushed into huge towers by the hot air coming up off the desert. I like the spectacular lightning. I like the winds. I'm still not all that crazy about dust storms, but I like the unpredictability of it all.

Is it going to be a dust storm or a gully-washer? Is it going to pour over a few blocks and leave the rest of the city dry, or is it going to rain everywhere? Will the streets flood? Will the lights just flicker and come right back or is the power off for the night? Is it ever going to end?

Let's face it: We don't get that much weather here. Maybe the occasional record high for the day. Maybe a sharp cold (for us) snap around Christmas. Every now and then some wavering from the norm.

Except for the monsoon: It's Show Time. It's muggy, it's unpredictable, it's big and mean and dangerous, and it seems to go on forever. By late September, early October, it has made everyone crabby.

But it's different, and it's interesting. And it's Arizonan. It may be rotten weather, but it's our rotten weather. Gol-durn it.

And it's something to complain about. You can't overlook the importance of whining for building community spirit.

Let the lotus-eaters go over to La Jolla to sit out the season on the beach.

Wimps.

I'm going over to Lois' house and sit out on the patio and watch the lightning.

Unless the streets are flooded.

Scare Tactics Could Solve Javelina Woes

September 7, 2001

Today's question: *We have a herd of javelinas that have decided to come down to a common area in our neighborhood directly behind our house and use it for a latrine. If you've never smelled javelina poop, it's something else. Is there anything that will repel these creatures? I tried mothballs already.*

Thank you for sharing your thoughts about javelina poop. I really wasn't hungry for lunch anyway.

I consulted on this one with Joe Yarchin, an urban wildlife specialist with the state Game and Fish Department. He knows all about stuff like this, although as far as I know he doesn't know who stole my bedspread off the clothesline the other day. This really honks me off. I bet it was javelinas.

Anyway, Yarchin said your best bet is a fence. You don't need to put up a great big block fence. Try driving some wrought-iron stakes deep into the ground and maybe reinforcing them with chicken wire.

You need to make sure there isn't anyone in the neighborhood putting food out for the javelinas because they think they're cute animals. I don't know why anyone would think they're cute, but some people do.

Some repellants based on red pepper might work short-term and you could try scattering around some rags that have been soaked in ammonia. It can't smell any worse than the javelinas. Yarchin said he doesn't like using mothballs because it just means that many more chemicals leaching into the soil.

Yarchin also said you should try to discourage them from getting comfortable. You could try spraying them with a hose, but I think they might actually like that. You can also run at them and wave your arms and shout. It's not like they're going to eat you or anything.

He also suggested making a shake can by sealing some pennies or small pebbles in a can and then winging it at the javelinas. It won't really hurt them, but it might scare them off. Let me know if you do that because it sort of sounds like fun.

Odd Ways To Hydrate Your Tree

December 7, 2001

I have in front of me a question from a lady who wants to know why Scotch tape won't stick to butter.

Why do you suppose she wants to know? What do you think she has been doing? Why would she want to tape butter? The mind boggles.

However, there is no time for such foolishness today, because we are going to take up the topic of Christmas traditions — caroling, exchanging gifts, visiting loved ones, baking cookies, throwing the Christmas tree into the swimming pool.

I had never heard of the last one until I got a letter from a woman whose husband wants to soak their Christmas tree in the pool for a couple of days before putting it up. She sounded quite worried about this.

I have never thrown a Christmas tree into a swimming pool, so I don't know what effect, if any, the needles would have on the pool filter.

Bob Khan, a deputy chief in the Phoenix Fire Department, has never thrown a Christmas tree into a pool either, but he has heard of the practice and said it's a good way to hydrate the tree before putting it up. Make a fresh cut on the end first.

Christmas trees are, of course, just big stacks of kindling waiting for a match, so anything you can do to keep them from drying up is good.

The traditional method of hacking a couple inches off the bottom and standing the tree in water isn't very helpful, Khan said, because in a couple of days the sap coagulates in the cut and the tree doesn't draw any water.

Khan has a new plan this year: Drill a hole an inch or so deep near the middle of the tree. Suspend a bag of water in the tree — the decorations will cover it — and then run a tube from the bag to the hole. Sap won't fill up the hole, and the tree will have a steady supply of water.

I don't know, but I'm guessing you could get something like an IV bag in the medical supplies section of a drug store.

Or maybe you could rig up a hot water bottle somehow. That might work.

You figure it out. I'm going to tape up some butter.

The Making Of Olive Oil Slippery Job

January 6, 2002

Today's question: *Being Canadian and never having seen real olive trees, I am delighted to find one on my daughter's property in Paradise Valley. What do you do with them? I have visions of dancing and crushing them beneath our callused Canadian feet for the first press of a famous new olive oil.*

One day last winter I wrote something mildly snarky about winter visitors and got calls and letters from grouchy snowbirds for days afterward.

With that in mind, we shall take up today's question without any such reflections.

However, it does behoove me to note that you don't get oil out of olives by dancing on them. Maybe you were thinking of grapes.

You get oil out of olives by squeezing them in some kind of a press. This is a long, complicated process.

In fact, almost anything concerning olives seems to involve a long, complicated process.

You would have to really want olives to deal with them yourself instead of just hopping down to the supermarket and buying some.

I asked the extremely helpful staff at the extremely helpful Cooperative Extension Agency (602-470-8086) about this, and they sent me eight pages of instructions on curing olives. Of course, that's far too much to print here, but let me just say this: lye.

The problem with olives is they are full of very bitter glucosides that have to be leached out to make them edible.

There are several ways of curing olives, but many of them involve soaking the fruit in lye or brine for several days.

In some cases you can crack the olives with a rolling pin and then soak them in cold water for 25 days, stirring frequently.

It sounds like a pretty tedious process, but if you really want to try it, call the Extension Service and ask them for the directions.

If you don't want to go to all the work, consider this: I know a guy who shoots olives at pigeons with a slingshot. That might be fun.

Emissions Test Is About Gunk, Not Gas

May 2, 2002

I just got a note from a guy who said his mother had sprayed a gecko with bug spray because she thought it was a scorpion. He said they've lived in Arizona only five days.

If you live near these people, I think the kind thing to do would be to go over there and have a little chat with them about things before they hurt themselves.

I'd go myself, but I'm pretty busy with questions such as this:

Can I increase my chances of passing the vehicle emissions test by filling up with premium gasoline before I go to the testing station?

Nope.

On the other hand, if you are using fuel with an octane rating well below what is recommended, it could conceivably hurt your chances of passing the test.

But Patrick Gibbons, spokesman for the state Department of Environmental Quality, said using a higher-than-usual octane rating won't make any difference.

Basically, the test is looking to find out how well your engine is running and how much gunk it is throwing off.

If your engine isn't performing properly at one octane rating, going to a higher level probably isn't going to make it any better, at least not in terms of emissions.

What you can do to improve your chances is make sure your car is running well. If you're not sure it will pass — in Phoenix, about 18 percent fail the first test — take it to your mechanic ahead of time. If it passes, fine. If not, you're going to end up hanging around the mechanic's place anyway while he explains that the framus on your gooboo was clogging up the bing-bang. No wonder your car failed.

Also, make sure your vehicle is completely warmed up, so the catalytic converter is working well, before you go in, and try not to run the air-conditioning. The AC increases the load on your engine.

Again, the best thing you can do is keep your car in good shape.

Remember: An ounce of framus is worth a pound of bing-bang.

Defining Lines In State Geography
August 18, 2002

It just occurred to me that I haven't used the word "goober" in a long time. Goober is a good word. It rolls off the tongue nicely. I'm going to have to find some excuse to use it soon.

This is by no means meant to suggest today's question came from a goober. Today's question is one that I get a lot actually, but this version came from a pair of innocent, fresh-faced newcomers with no whiff of gooberocity about them.

We're confused. What's the difference between the Mogollon Rim and the White Mountains?

Did you know Arizona law contains a legal description of the Rim? They wrote it when they were setting the boundaries for the Fort Apache reservation.

It's pretty long, but this is the first sentence: *The cliff-like escarpment located in northern Arizona which separates the Colorado plateau and the central highlands and forms, in part, the divide between the little Colorado river and Salt river drainage areas, also forming a portion of the boundaries of Coconino and Gila counties, is designated and shall be known as the "Mogollon Rim."*

The rest of it is a lot of longitude and latitude and other stuff that would just confuse you. Or at least it confused me.

Geologically, the Mogollon Rim is an erosional escarpment that marks the southern edge of the Mogollon Plateau and runs southeast from around Flagstaff into New Mexico.

However, you can't see a lot of the southeast end of it because that part is covered up by the White Mountains.

The White Mountains are a collection of volcanic peaks — Mount Baldy, for instance — in eastern Arizona. They run roughly from the Fort Apache Reservation into the Apache National Forest.

They were sometimes known as the Mogollon Mountains, but the Spanish explorers referred to them as the Sierra Blanca.

Look at it like this. Payson is just under the Mogollon Rim. Alpine is in the White Mountains. It would be nice to be there today.

I could go on, but I see a pack of my masters roaming the newsroom, and I'm going to slip out. Those goobers.

Bar Story Beats Truth Of Border

September 14, 2003

Why does Arizona's southern border slant off to the northwest instead of running straight east and west?

There is a very good reason for this, according to Marshall Trimble, state historian and swell guy.

After the Gadsden Purchase of 1853, surveyors were laying out the new boundary, working from east to west. When they came to Nogales, they discovered the closest bar was in Yuma, so they headed there directly, marking the border as they went.

This, of course, is not true. However, as Trimble pointed out, it makes for a better story than what really happened.

In 1848, at the end of the Mexican War, Mexico gave up a huge hunk of territory including parts of what are now New Mexico, Arizona, California, Colorado, Utah and Nevada, plus its claim to Texas. The southern border of Arizona at the time was the Gila River.

However, a few years later we decided we needed more, and James Gadsden, our ambassador to Mexico, negotiated the purchase of 45,535 square miles of what is now southern bits of Arizona and New Mexico for $10 million.

There were two reasons for this. One, some Americans believed we had snookered Mexico over that whole war business, and this was seen as a way of making it up to them. Secondly, and more important, we wanted the land for the route of a southern transcontinental railroad that would be usable year-round.

According to Trimble, Southern interests wanted us to buy a much larger piece of land from Mexico. Northern interests, worried about the South being too big, argued for buying just enough for the railroad.

And Mexico didn't want to lose its land route to Baja California, fearing that if it did the Americans in California would just move in.

Eventually, the Northern interests prevailed and instead of buying up the head of the Gulf of California and all that other land, we got Yuma.

Squabbling Good For Business
February 1, 2004

Today we have two questions about desert matters from squabbling couples.

Now don't get me wrong: I wish you all long and happy marriages. But I have to say, these little spats are certainly good for business.

Here goes:

My wife and I have been disagreeing about this for years. It has consumed our lives. Is there quicksand in Arizona?

Consumed their lives? Geez.

Yes, there is quicksand in Arizona. Not a lot, I suppose, because we're so dry, but it is not at all unusual to find quicksand along the banks of an Arizona stream or at a place where water might be flowing underground, like along the Hassayampa River or some place like that.

Quicksand basically is sand floating on water. The water reduces the friction between the grains of sand to the point where the mixture cannot support much weight and you get bogged down in it.

If you did happen to get stuck in quicksand, your chances of really getting sucked under are slim because it generally isn't all that deep. Stay calm, make slow movements and you'll just kind of float in the stuff. Thrash around a lot and you'll just make it worse. Come to think of it, staying calm, moving slowly and not thrashing around so much is pretty good advice for much of life.

I say the desert is just sand and dirt and rocks and desert plants, but my husband claims he read somewhere that it is really covered with a hard crust that you can fall through. What's he talking about?

You people. When you go hiking, don't you ever stop and look around at stuff? Like the ground?

OK, in many areas the desert is covered with a thin layer of rocks or stuff, and it's easy to get your car stuck when the wheels break through that shell and spin in the sand underneath.

But what I think your husband is talking about is the desert's cryptobiotic crust, which is common in desert areas.

The cryptobiotic crust is made up of soil particles bound together by organic materials like bacteria, really tiny fungi, algae, mosses and lichens and things of that nature. It is very important and very delicate stuff, which is why you're supposed to stay on the trails when you hike and not just go gallivanting off where you feel like going.

The cryptobiotic crust reduces erosion, helps hold water in the soil and also fixes nitrogen and carbon out of the atmosphere and adds them to the soil.

So keep your eyes open, stay on the trail and don't thrash so much.

Knowledge About Coyotes
May 7, 2004

I live in the East Valley near Usery Mountain Park. There are a lot of coyotes that hang out in my neighborhood. However, I can't figure out where they get their water. As far as I know, any canals or rivers are miles away, the washes are dry, and all the pools are fenced off. So where do they get their water?

I wonder if this person is a newcomer. He didn't say.

Sounds a bit like it to me, though.

I'm pretty sure tomorrow's question is from a newcomer, too. Wait till you hear it.

Newcomer or not, I think this is a pretty interesting question, mostly because I think coyotes are pretty interesting animals.

We all know that as the cities expand and the desert shrinks and the drought continues we have more coyotes coming into urban areas.

But I read something interesting while checking out this water thing: Most coyotes will live out their lives without ever seeing a human being.

I wonder if that's true.

If it is, that's pretty cool.

So, about water. First of all, like a lot of desert animals, coyotes can make do without or with very little for longer than you might think. Kit foxes can thrive with no "free" water at all. They get what they need from the stuff they eat.

And while it might seem like all the pools are fenced, there are plenty of dog water bowls, irrigation ditches, stock tanks, natural seeps, park ponds and golf-course water hazards around if you know where to look for them, and coyotes know where to look for them.

And everything a coyote eats — from mice to your cat — has some moisture in it, and coyotes are adapted to make the most of it.

I didn't know this before: In the deserts of Arizona, Mexico and California there are certain gourds called buffalo gourds or calabazillas or loco melons. But they are also known as coyote gourds because coyotes dine on them, not just for the food but also for the moisture they hold.

The flesh of these gourds is said to taste awful, but Native Americans used to eat the seeds.

Last but not least, coyotes also are known to get water by digging "wells," especially around mesquite trees, which have very deep taproots.

So I wouldn't worry about the coyotes dying of thirst if I were you.

They're coyotes.

They know what they're doing.

How your body works, when it does...

Psalm 139 tells us we are awesomely and wondrously made. I guess this must be so.

I know in my own case that I have noticed lately that the abdominal pieces of my own particular body have grown to be distinctively awesome in an awesomely jiggly kind of way while the hair on my head, which was once as thick as a bale of straw, has become distinctly unwondrous.

This is sort of awesome and wondrous in its own way, I suppose. But why is it that God or nature or whatever arranges it so that with age the waistline gets larger and the hair gets thinner? Why can't it be the other way around? Like, the older we get, the better looking we get. That would seem to be fair. We've earned it. Nobody seems to know why this can't be so.

Anyway, I think that's why this is really my favorite part of this book — the part about the human body and the functions of the human body and the peculiarities of the human body and so on. Those other parts aren't so bad, I guess, and I hope you liked them, but I'm thinking now this is really the highlight of this whole collection. Or this whole mess, as the case may be.

It's my favorite because of that part about nobody knowing for sure about so much stuff. I mean, it's our bodies. Bodies we've been walking around in for millions of years, and using to do ordinary sort of everyday stuff for millions of years. But still nobody knows why we do some of that stuff, like yawning or getting the hiccups, or why looking at a bright light makes some people sneeze and just makes other people squint. Or like why even bald people have dandruff. I mean, we seem to have figured out the human body right down to the to the gene that makes old people drive around for miles with their turn signal on, but we still don't know for sure why we yawn. You'd think we would have figured out some of that sort of stuff by now, but we haven't. I think that's sort of cool. If we knew everything about ordinary stuff like yawning or sneezing, it wouldn't be so interesting, don't you think?

Meanwhile, there is lots of stuff about our bodies we do know. Why fat ladies make such good opera singers. Why our teeth chatter when we're cold. Why paper cuts hurt so much. Why you get all wrinkly if you stay in the bathtub long enough. That's all fairly awesome and wondrous, if you ask me. I just wish my abdominal parts were a little less awesomely jiggly and my hair parts were a tad more wondrous.

Heating Up: Go Ahead and Shiver
January 26, 2001

Why do my teeth chatter when I'm cold?

Off the top of my head, I'd say it's because you're a wuss. Granted, it's a bit on the cool side, but it's not that cold.

Of course, it's possible you've been up in the mountains or someplace where it's really cold, and that's when your teeth were chattering.

Your teeth were chattering because the Second (or so) Law of Thermodynamics says heat flows from a warm object to a cold object. In other words, you're losing body heat and getting cold.

When you're cold, your old pal, your body, starts telling you to please put on a jacket or something for heaven's sake or to go inside, and in the meantime it's trying to warm itself up by shivering. It's possible for your body to shiver you so hard that your teeth rattle, or at least chatter.

Shivering and teeth-chattering generate heat from the increase in chemical reactions necessary for muscle activity. It is possible for your body to crank up heat production by as much as 500 percent by shivering, but this won't keep you warm very long because sooner or later your shivering muscles get tired.

So usually, it's just that. You shiver and chatter because your body is trying to get warm by exercising, and sooner or later you put on a sweater or turn up the heat or whatever, and everything is fine.

However, shivering and chattering also can mark the onset of hypothermia, which of course is a very nasty thing indeed.

You don't have to be lost in a blizzard to get hit by hypothermia.

Depending on the wind and moisture and other conditions, hypothermia can sneak up on you even if the air temperature is as high as the 50s or 60s.

So be careful. Take an extra sweater or something when you go hiking, especially this time of year. Listen to your teeth.

Overcoming Stress? Try Aimless Sloth
April 20, 2001

I can't believe this newspaper. These people have the news judgment of stumps.

On Wednesday, Reuters news service moved one of the most significant, exciting news stories I have ever read. I was sure it would be on the front page Thursday, but no. Not one word.

I would have missed it myself had not my eagle-eyed colleague E.J. Montini passed it on to me, which wasn't hard to do since I was lying on the couch next to his cubicle at the time. I was thinking.

I wish I had enough room here to print this incredibly important story in its entirety. Here are the highlights:

Peter Axt, a German college professor and health researcher, has concluded that "aimless sloth" is the secret to overcoming stress and living a long life.

Aimless sloth! Is that great or what? That would make such a cool tattoo.

Axt acknowledges that a healthy diet and moderate exercise, such as leisurely walks, are good for you.

However, he said: "Research shows that people who run long distances into their 50s are using up energy they need for other purposes."

"They suffer memory loss. They risk premature senility."

Memory loss! Premature senility! I'm nominating this guy for a Nobel Prize.

"People who would rather laze in a hammock instead of running a marathon or who take a midday nap instead of playing squash have a better chance of living into old age," Axt said.

I think he may have gone a little overboard there. I think hammocks are dangerous.

Axt has published his findings in a study called "On the Joy of Laziness." His previous works include "Just Stay Young" and "Eat Yourself Slim."

This is Axt's prescription for a long and healthy life: "Waste half your free time."

The man is a god.

Black-Robed Folks Know What's Cool

May 9, 2001

We are always told to wear light-colored clothing when exercising or hiking in hot weather. So why do I always see pictures of people in the Sahara wearing big, dark robes that cover them from head to foot?

Hmm, that's a good question. I prefer it greatly to the question from the lady who wants to know what's wrong with her amaryllis plant, because amaryllis is much too hard to spell.

I even did some actual research on this question and came up with some actual explanations which — hold on to your hats here — might actually be true.

Any grade-school science student knows that dark cloth absorbs more heat than white cloth because it soaks up more of the light spectrum. So why are Bedouins walking around the desert in those great big loose-fitting, dark robes? Such a robe is, by the way, called a burnoose. I wonder where you get one. I bet I'd look cool in a burnoose.

Anyway, I found one study in which researchers found the surface of a black burnoose was 11 degrees hotter than the surface of a white robe. However, when they measured the skin temperature of the test subject, it was the same whether he had on the black burnoose or the white one.

The theory is that the warm air trapped beneath the black robe and the wearer's skin rose faster than the air under the white robe. This would create enough of a breeze to keep you feeling cool.

I also found a study that determined if there is any kind of breeze, loose-fitting black clothing will keep you cooler than loose-fitting white clothes. That's because the white might reflect sunlight away, but it also bounces internal heat back toward your body, while black clothing absorbs both the sunlight and the body heat. So all things being equal, a breeze would transfer the heat away faster from the guy in the black robe.

To Cool Off Outside, Get Hot Inside

May 29, 2001

My husband insists that eating hot, spicy food during hot weather actually helps you cool off. He is wrong about so many other things. Please tell him he is wrong about this. I think he's going to give himself a stroke.

Sorry, lady. He got this one right. Why do you think a lot of spicy dishes come from hot places, such as Mexico or Thailand or India? Ever think of that? Huh?

When you eat spicy food all sorts of things happen. Your body decides to cool off. Blood vessels close to the surface of your skin, especially on your face and neck, expand so the blood can throw off heat. Your internal temperature goes down while your skin temperature goes up. You sweat, and as the sweat evaporates it cools you off.

And the longer you live in hot weather, the better your body gets at doing all that. That's why when it's cold around here, you hear people saying their blood has thinned out. Your body is just used to cooling off, not warming up.

It's kind of the reverse of why drinking alcohol isn't a good idea in hot weather. Aside from the fact it makes you stupid, alcohol constricts your blood vessels so it's harder for your body to carry heat out from your insides.

So, amazing as it may be, your husband is apparently right about this one. Don't feel bad. As you said, he's probably wrong about plenty of other things.

While we're on the subject, do you know why water never seems to help if you've just set your mouth on fire with a big bite of spicy food?

Because a lot of spicy foods have a lot of oil in them and are often cooked in oil. It coats your lips and tongue and throat, and since oil and water don't mix, that big glass of ice water you just swallowed doesn't wash away the hot stuff. Milk works and so does alcohol, but if neither of those appeal, a piece of bread or a tortilla will smother the flames.

Another Clue About Temperature
August 4, 2001

I am writing on behalf of my 6-year-old daughter. She asked me this after watching the vet take our dog's temperature. This is her question, but not in these exact words: "If our internal temperature is 98.6 degrees, why are we uncomfortable when the temperature outside is that hot? Shouldn't we be cold at anything less than 98.6 and only hot when the temperature passes this point?"

Couldn't you have just made something up? That's what I always do when my kids ask me hard questions. So they think there are little tiny rich people in the ATM machines who count the money and hand it out to you. Big deal. They're turning out OK.

OK, perch your little daughter on your knee and I shall make it all clear.

Yes indeed, the normal body temperature is 98.6 degrees. That's our optimum operating temperature. However, your body really has to work at it to keep itself at or near that temperature. To keep from overheating, your body throws off excess heat into the air. It's like a car engine. You have to put coolant in it or it will overheat and the parts will melt.

And, when two objects touch — two objects such as you and the air around you — the rate of heat flow from one to another depends on the temperature difference between the two objects. OK? If you're outside in freezing weather the heat flows rapidly from you to the surrounding air and your body temperature drops. If the temperature outside was 98.6 degrees, there would be no flow of heat and your body temperature would keep going up because of the heat it generated.

So we need to be surrounded by air that is cool enough to keep the heat flowing away from our bodies at about the same rate we crank it out. For most of us, that's about 72 degrees.

OK? Tell your daughter that. If she still doesn't understand it, tell her to ask the little man in the ATM machine.

Jiggling Eye, Illusion Cited For Tire Spin

November 17, 2001

Why do the wheels of cars appear to be rotating backward in motion pictures or TV ads?

I'm glad you asked. I always wondered about that, too, and I'd been meaning to look it up.

There is a question here of whether or not this is an optical illusion, such as a warm, friendly smile from one of my masters. We will get to that in a minute.

The reason the stagecoach wheel or the car wheels or the airplane propellers seem to be rotating backward in the movies or on TV has to do with the speed at which the film was shot and the speed at which the wheel is turning.

If there were exactly one rotation of the wheel for every one snapshot, every frame of film, it would look like the wheel was not moving at all. If the wheel is rotating slightly slower than the frame rate, it will look like it was going backward because the wheel isn't making a full rotation for each frame shot. If the wheel is rotating faster than the film is being shot, it would look like it was rotating slowly forward.

It's kind of like watching somebody dance while strobe lights are flashing. Your eyes and your brain only capture certain moments of the movements. This is called a stroboscopic effect.

The question is this: Is this an optical illusion or not? One source I found said a stroboscopic effect is not an optical illusion because your brain is actually registering what your eyes are seeing.

To my mind, an optical illusion is when you see something differently than it really is, and the backward wheel thing certainly is different than it really is.

I also found another source that said the backward-rotation effect is caused by your eyeballs "jiggling...commonly due to eating crunchy foods." This is called oscillopsia.

However, if your eyeballs jiggle when you eat crunchy foods, I don't want to hear about it. And besides, oscillopsia is too hard to spell.

No One Really Knows Why We Yaaawwn

January 4, 2002

Why do we yawn, anyway? What's the point?

This is a very good question, because no one knows the answer for sure, which means I can blather on about it at great length and not get it wrong. Probably.

Almost all animals yawn, even reptiles. Human fetuses as young as 11 weeks have been seen yawning. Even ants yawn. I didn't know that before.

But no one knows exactly why we yawn.

One theory is that we yawn because when we are tired or bored or not moving around much our breathing slows, and we yawn to take in a big gulp of oxygen and blow out the carbon dioxide that has been building up. However, they've tested people in atmospheres that are oxygen-rich and in rooms with extra carbon dioxide and they didn't yawn any more or less than usual.

Also that theory doesn't explain why you sometimes see athletes yawn just before a big game or a race or something. You certainly wouldn't expect them to be bored or tired.

Another idea is that it is just a way of stretching your lungs and your face muscles. Lots of people stretch when they yawn. It increases your blood pressure and heart rate and flexes your muscles.

The interesting part about yawning is that no one knows why it seems to be contagious. You're probably yawning right now. Fifty-five percent of people will yawn within five minutes of seeing someone else yawn, according to one study I found, and blind people will yawn after listening to a tape of someone yawning.

One theory is that the contagious thing is a leftover from evolution, that way back on the family tree our ancestors yawned to signal to the rest of the pack that it was time to go to sleep or time to change activities and everyone else yawned to show agreement.

Sneezing: The Fast And The Furious
February 13, 2002

Why is it that placing an index finger under your nose horizontally keeps you from sneezing? Or at least it always seemed to work on Gilligan's Island.

Did you know some people get turned on by sneezing? Like there's a whole sneeze fetish thing going on? Ewww. This is just one of many weird things I learned in the course of looking up the answer to this question.

A good sneeze is your body's way of cleaning out the ductwork with a blast of high-pressure air. When the nerve endings in your mucous membranes are irritated by dust or pollen or germs or something, they set off a kind of full-body workout. Your breathing muscles inhale deeply and then close off the airways so the air pressure in your lungs rises. When the pressure is great enough, the airways snap open and a big burst of air shoots out your nose. A sneeze can send air out your nose at 100 mph and can spread germs and goo and other stuff for 12 feet.

The main nerve involved here is the fifth cranial nerve, the trigeminal nerve, which has nerve endings all over your face. If you press your finger under your nose you might temporarily block the nerve impulse and stave off the sneeze until you can get to a tissue or a handkerchief.

Bright light can make about 25 percent of people sneeze, but researchers aren't sure why. One theory is that there is some sort of association between the optic nerve and the trigeminal nerve and that when the optic nerve reacts to bright light, it sets off some response in the trigeminal nerve. Another idea is that when you squint in bright light, it pushes fluid from the lacrimal sac (tears) down into your nose, and that makes you sneeze.

And the reason you can't sneeze with your eyes open is because of the tremendous air pressure that builds up in your head before you let rip. Your eyelids slam shut to keep your eyeballs from shooting out of the sockets, which would be nothing to sneeze at.

Coffee Hour Yields Final Authority

April 23, 2002

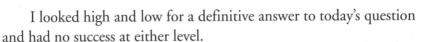

I looked high and low for a definitive answer to today's question and had no success at either level.

So I was forced to submit the matter to the court of last resort: the People at the Coffee Hour at Church.

The People at the Coffee Hour at Church are a varied lot and know all sorts of stuff. Some of it may even be true. They all seemed to be pretty much unanimous about their answer, so there is a pretty good chance it is correct.

This is the question:

Why doesn't someone who snores very loudly wake himself or herself up with the noise?

It is not uncommon, if you are a snorer, to jolt yourself awake with a snort just as you are dozing off, but why isn't the snorer aroused from a deep sleep by the sound? The same person might be awakened by a baby's cry or a ringing phone but not that ungodly racket going off right in his or her own head.

So I asked the People at the Coffee Hour at Church, and they couldn't believe I was too dumb to figure it out, although most of them have known me awhile and should have a pretty good idea about that by now.

It is the considered opinion of the People at the Coffee Hour at Church that snoring is just a background noise that the snorer simply tunes out and does not hear. It's like being accustomed to urban night noises so you can sleep through sirens and so forth. Or like being exposed for a long time to a foul odor; after a while you just don't smell it.

The People at the etc., etc., also opined that people who snore and who are afflicted with apnea, the temporary cessation of breathing, are awakened not by snores but by the lack of breath. That makes sense, I guess.

Hypnic Jerk: A Bedtime Peculiarity

June 20, 2002

I have here two sleep-related questions that you seem to be worrying about.

I know I've told you this before, but you people worry entirely too much. If you ate more pie and listened to more baseball on the radio, you wouldn't worry so much. And your skin might clear up, too.

Why is that when you're just drifting off to sleep you suddenly feel like you're falling and all your muscles seem to jerk at once?

This is a called a hypnic or a myoclonic jerk. It happens to about 80 percent of us.

The reasons it happens are a bit fuzzy. I found one source that speculated that as you fall asleep and your breathing slows and your temperature drops a bit, your brain decides you're dying so it sends out a sort of a jump-start just to see if you're OK. That doesn't sound like much of a theory to me.

Most people who know about these matters say they don't know about this one. They're guessing it is some kind of disturbance in the brain function. It's no big deal, unless it happens over and over and over again in the same night every night, in which case you should see a doctor.

What's the deal with sleepy seeds?

It took me awhile to figure out what this reader was asking about, until I realized she meant eye boogers. Those are those little bits of crust you sometimes find in the corner of your eyelid in the morning.

Your eyes are always making tears to keep the eyeball moist and fed. Tears are made up of salty water, proteins and fat. Eye boogers are the proteins and fat from dried-up tears.

At night, after you've stopped myoclonic jerking around and you're finally asleep, your eyes are shut. So they don't need tears to rinse away any dirt, and you're not crying in your sleep, so the tears dry up and leave behind those little crusty boogers.

If you are crying while you're sleeping, you have what they call "issues" and should eat more pie.

Soak This One Up: You're A Sponge

October 24, 2002

I just got a note from a guy who wants to know why we can't print the ads for ladies underwear in color.

You people.

However, this has nothing to do with today's question, which is one that comes in fairly often and one that I'm pretty sure I did once before. But what the heck, anything to further the education of a small child.

My little daughter was playing in the tub and asked me, "Mommy, why do my fingers turn white and wrinkly and squishy from the water?" I said, "Honey, let's ask Clay Thompson." Can you help?

That's not a very good parenting policy, if you ask me. You can't go through life saying to your children, "Honey, let's ask Clay Thompson," whenever they ask you a hard question. What are you going to say when they ask you where babies come from or if you smoked dope when you were younger or if they can have the keys to the car? Honey, let's ask Clay Thompson? Forget it. You're on your own.

However, I will bail you out this time because it's an easy one.

OK, you've got two layers of skin, the epidermis on top and the dermis under that. The epidermis produces some oily stuff called sebum, which is what leaves your greasy fingerprints on stuff. Sebum also keeps water out of your skin.

If you are in the water a long time, this sebum gets washed away and you start taking on water.

That lower level of skin contains a lot of the protein keratin, which soaks up water like a sponge.

The two layers of skin are connected at certain points. As the lower level swells with water at the points where they are not connected, the skin wrinkles.

When you get out of the tub, the water evaporates and your body starts greasing you up with sebum again and your skin goes back to normal.

The skin on your hands and feet, which gets a lot of wear and tear, is thicker than the skin on the rest of your body and soaks up water more easily. That's why the rest of you doesn't get all wrinkly in the tub.

Any more questions, kids? Go ask your mom.

Big Voice, Big Body: It All Works
November 28, 2002

Are you having a good Thanksgiving? I hope so.

I hope you are not having one of those Thanksgivings where, before you can eat, you all have to go around the table and tell everyone else what you are thankful for. If you do, you know you're probably either going to sound like a weenie or a gomer or maybe even a pervert, and the pervert thing is probably going to put everyone else off their feed. Meanwhile, the stuffing is getting cold, and that's the best part.

Myself, I am thankful for today's question, which is one of those things I always kind of wondered about, but I never thought to check out.

We've all heard the expression "It's not over until the fat lady sings." But why are opera singers always fat?

I think "big-boned" or maybe "husky" would be a little bit more genteel than "fat," don't you?

On the other hand, there is no denying than many stars of the opera seem to be...um, good eaters. Have you ever seen Cecilia Bartoli? Well, so what of it? Don't be putting the bad mouth on Cecilia Bartoli. I have a major case of the hots for Cecilia Bartoli, and she's not fat. She's just gifted. And look at Kiri Te Kanawa. You wouldn't call her fat, would you? Healthy, maybe, but not fat.

Some opera heavyweights, no pun intended, do give the impression they have been putting away the alfredo sauce by the gallon. Look at Luciano Pavarotti. He ain't exactly Leonardo Di Caprio, is he?

But it doesn't seem to be their intake of calories so much as maybe their born-with build that makes opera greats great. Plus, of course, the God-given gifts of voice and music and the years of hard work of training and controlling that voice.

A lot of it has to do with your voice box, your larynx. We all have one, but if you happen to have one that has a lot of fat around it, you might be in luck, singing-wise. It's thought that maybe some extra fat around your larynx gives you more vibes, more resonance, in your voice.

Here's another thing: If you're an opera singer and you're up there trying to be heard all the way to the end of the hall over the orchestra and the coughing and whatnot from the audience — like guys whispering, "Can we leave at intermission?" — you need a pretty good set of pipes. Actually, you need a major set of pipes.

And if you are a person of, shall we say, some stature, you will probably come equipped with a good-sized diaphragm and a good-sized chest cavity that will give you the power to really belt it out, if you also come blessed with the gift of music.

Or you might just be a good eater. For today, at least, I hope so.

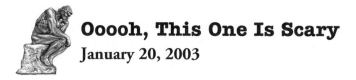

Ooooh, This One Is Scary
January 20, 2003

Can you explain what goose bumps are all about? Sometimes we get them when we're cold, but I've also had them in response to a touch or fear or a sound, like a beautiful passage of music.

You get goose bumps at the sound of beautiful music? That's nice. You must be a sensitive and refined person. Well, of course you are, or you wouldn't be reading this column, would you then? Personally, I get goose bumps at the sound of my masters' voices, which tend to be raspy and guttural, accompanied by the occasional high-pitched whine. Sometimes they just grunt and point, especially when eating.

Goose bumps are pretty interesting. The technical word for them is horripilation, which comes in part from the Latin word *horrere*, which means something really scary, like something that might make your hair stand on end, which is pretty much what's going on when you get goose bumps.

If you are scared or cold, your involuntary nervous system fires off a message to a bunch of little muscles called the *arrectores pilorum* telling them to contract. When they do, they lift the hair follicles above the rest of the skin, and you are all goose-bumpy.

That's not all that's going on. You are also getting lubed. When your hair stands up, the follicle presses down on a small gland under your skin that then releases some oil to keep your skin from drying out. Meanwhile, to save heat, the ducts of your sweat glands and the blood vessels near the surface of your skin are contracting. And you might also have a good shiver to get yourself warmed up.

Isn't it interesting that your body does all those complicated things all at once and all on its own, but it still doesn't tell you when you have a piece of spinach stuck on your teeth? You would think it could be more considerate about things like that.

The goose bump thing is probably a throwback to long ago, eons ago, when we were hairier and puffing up all that hair would make us look big and scary. Haven't you ever seen a cat that's had a fright? Its hair stands up and it looks bigger than it really is. Same thing.

What is less clear is why we get goose bumps over something we don't perceive as scary or when we're not cold, like this woman who gets goose bumps at the sound of beautiful music.

This would be my guess: Maybe something like that — music or a lover's kiss or really good barbecue — or something else sweet and beautiful is just so wonderful that you can't comprehend it. You are awed, which I guess you could say is a form of fear, so you get goose bumps.

Just a guess.

Working Up Sweat Over Perspiration
January 23, 2003

Can elephants swim?

Yes.

Hmm. Well, I guess that settles that. What shall we talk about now?

Is it true that babies born in desert areas have or develop more sweat glands than ones born in, say, the Midwest? Since our family has both, which of us is better prepared for summer?

Let me get this straight: You have a child born in the Midwest and a child born in Arizona and you want to know if the desert child has more sweat glands than the Midwestern child? Where do you people get these ideas?

Everyone is born with a set number of sweat glands, somewhere between 2 million and 4 million, and scientists think that maybe nobody has the same number as anyone else. I don't know how they know that.

Genetics, I suppose, might play some role in determining how many sweat glands you get. However, the idea that maybe after you've lived here a few summers, you and your spouse are going to pass on more sweat glands to your baby is pretty much hooey. Did your desert baby arrive already coated with sunscreen and clutching a water bottle?

Babies sweat, but most sweat glands don't kick in until puberty. That's why teenagers are smellier than little kids.

Humans have two kinds of sweat glands, eccrine and apocrine.

Eccrine glands are all over the place — between 150 and 340 per square centimeter of skin. Did you know there are no sweat glands on your eardrums? That's just as well, I suppose.

Apocrine glands are the ones in your armpits and crotch. Apocrine sweat is smellier than eccrine sweat. The smell comes from bacteria on your skin reacting to the stuff the sweat glands throw off. The output of apocrine glands is closely related to some sex hormones.

Maybe I should have stuck with the elephants. They can swim up to 20 miles a day. That would be worth seeing.

Can You Stomach The Pain?
April 9, 2003

Today's question, according to the questioner, comes out of a dinner-table discussion involving three lawyers and an engineer.

That sounds like the start of a good joke, doesn't it? Three lawyers and an engineer are having dinner and…. It probably would be even funnier if it involved a talking cow.

While we're on the subject, did I ever tell you about my idea for a punch-line contest? The idea was to find the best punch line for a dirty joke that was not in itself dirty. Like, "I don't know. I never looked." Or, "That's not what the midget said." Anyway, my masters wouldn't let me do it. I suppose they were worried that it may have been fun.

However, no time for such fiddle-faddle now. We have to get to the lawyer/engineer question.

Does it hurt to have your belly button pierced? We have two schools of thought: that the belly button is either a nerveless remnant of a nutrition delivery system or it's more sensitive than many other body parts.

My own belly button — it's a cute little one, if I do say so myself — is not pierced, so I cannot speak to this matter from personal experience. However, I have conducted extensive research, mostly by wandering around the office asking people if they have pierced navels. If you are not a trained, professional researcher, such as myself, I do not recommend this technique, especially with your more sensitive female colleagues.

So anyway, the answer is, yes, it hurts. The degree to which it hurts apparently varies and depends on the skill of the piercer and the pain threshold of the piercee.

It was described to me in terms ranging from "a mild pin prick" to "a lot, really a lot."

Overall, however, I'm thinking it can't hurt that much or you wouldn't see so many pierced navels around.

If you are going to have your navel pierced — and God only knows why you would want to do that, but I guess it's not my business — have it done by a reputable, trained piercer. In other words, not your best friend's cousin who did her own one day when her parents weren't home. And follow carefully the post-piercing care instructions or you might end up with an infected belly button, which sounds extremely gross, if you ask me.

Nature Hedges Its Bets
April 19, 2003

Was this one of those weeks with about 11 days in it or what? Or was that just my imagination? It just seemed to go on forever. I don't know why for sure. It just did.

Whatever. It's Saturday now and it's the weekend, and my masters are far away doing whatever sort of hideous things they do on their weekends — their poor pets — and we are free to take up a question that seems to come in all the time. I don't know why this is such a matter of concern to you people, but it seems to be.

Why do men have nipples?

I am told that male horses and platypuses don't have nipples. This may or may not be true. I have never had occasion to check a male horse or platypus for nipples. I don't believe, come to think of it, that I have ever even seen a platypus outside of an encyclopedia.

Did you know that female opossums have anywhere from seven to 25 nipples, depending on what particular style of opossum you might have at hand? Neither did I until I started checking out this question. Doesn't it seem sort of strange to you to have an odd number of such body parts? There is probably a perfectly good reason for this. I just don't know what it is. I wouldn't worry about it if I were you.

However, we are not here to discuss opossums, which, personally, I find to be a rather creepy kind of animal. We are here to discuss humans, specifically human males and nipples.

This is the deal: You are a mammal. If you are reading this and you are not a mammal, you need to call the city desk as soon as possible and we will have a photographer and reporter out there right away, and your relatives will want to buy 20 copies of tomorrow's paper.

For the first 14 or so weeks you were in your mother's womb looking like a gooey lump of cells or whatever, it had not yet been decided yet if you would be a boy or a girl and obviously you didn't have anything to say about it. It could have gone either way.

Around 14 weeks or so, certain hormones kicked in and sorted out your chromosomes, that whole XX or XY thing, and decided if you would be someone who liked wandering around in hardware stores humming to yourself or if you would be beautiful and mysterious and not have a hairy back.

In the meantime, that lump of cells hedged its bets and gave you nipples just in case you might need them for something later. Good plan.

Decisions were made about the rest of your body parts later as things progressed, but the nipple issue needed to be settled early on.

Warning: This Query Is Morbid

May 16, 2003

I just got a phone message from a guy who wanted to know what my phone number is. In other words, he called my phone number, which is printed at the end of this column pretty much every day, to find out what it is.

Do you find this a bit, I don't know, odd? Or is it just me?

Think about this for a while and then we shall turn to today's question.

Can you get cancer of the heart? I've heard of brain cancer, liver cancer, stomach cancer, etc., but never heart cancer. Why is that?

This is not a good question. For one thing, it involves many words that are hard to spell.

For another thing, it is morbid. You can't think of enough things that might kill you without thinking about cancer of the heart?

Let's stop for a moment then to sort of lighten up and hear a joke one of you recently sent me.

Have you heard about the new pirate movie that's coming out?

It's rated arrrrrrrghrrr.

This, if you ask me, is not a particularly good joke, but it will have to do. I wonder if the person who sent it to me is related to the person who phoned to ask for my phone number. However, it is better than talking about new, treacherous ways your body will find to betray you, and it is more suitable than the other pirate joke I heard the other day, which involved a pirate and a steering wheel and cannot be printed here.

Anyway, yes, it is possible to get cancer of the heart — knock on wood — and should this happen you are going to be one very sorry pirate indeed.

I read somewhere that Eric Carr, who was a drummer for Kiss, died of heart cancer, but I don't know for a fact that this is true.

Heart cancer is known as primary cardiac sarcoma. It is very rare. I am told it turns up in something like 0.01 percent to 0.28 percent of autopsies in cancer deaths.

Primary cardiac sarcoma can take many forms, most of which are, as noted above, hard to spell: rhabdomyosarcomas, liposarcomas, osteosarcoma, neurogic sarcoma, leiomyosarcoma, synovial sarcoma, fibrosarcoma.

Trust me, you don't want to know.

It might be a cancer that spreads from another part of the body, or it might originate in the heart, often in the right atrium. If so, chances are that if it doesn't kill you by causing heart failure, it will spread quickly to your lungs and spine and find a way to kill you in one of those places.

That's enough about that. It is my theory that reading or talking about such things is bad luck. Stay healthy, mateys. Ask me more cheerful questions, but don't call to ask my phone number.

Arrrrrrghrr.

Getting A Charge From Foil
July 2, 2003

I have a note from a gentleman who wonders if there are such things as dog aliens. He reasons that dog aliens would have an easier time reaching us from another planet because they would travel not in light-years but in light-dog-years.

I am pretty sure this is a joke, but I never can be quite sure with you people.

Let us instead take up today's question:

Why do your teeth hurt when you chew on tin foil?

My teeth don't hurt when I chew on tin foil. There are two very good reasons why this is true. First of all, I make it a practice not to chew on foil because it would make my teeth hurt. Secondly, it is not tin foil. It is aluminum foil. Ergo, chewing on tin foil does not make my teeth hurt.

Perhaps, however, the questioner or others among you do chew on foil. Why you would want to do that, I couldn't say.

So this is why chewing on foil hurts your mouth — because you are old. I'm sorry to be the one to tell you this, but it can't be helped. You are old, and you have old fillings, probably silver. If you didn't have any fillings or if you are younger and have modern non-metallic fillings, chances are that chewing foil will not hurt your teeth, although, again, I can't imagine why you would want to go around chewing aluminum foil in the first place.

Anyway, this is what happens: When you chew a piece of foil, you are more or less turning your mouth into a wet, toothy battery. The aluminum provides one electrode and the metal filling is the other electrode, and all that saliva acts as an electrolyte solution to help pass the charge.

The current flows from the aluminum to the metal filling, which more than likely is nestled right up against the nerve ending in your tooth. It's a very small charge, but it's enough to hurt very, very much.

This is why I join with leading dentists and mothers everywhere to recommend that you do not chew on aluminum foil.

This, however, does not explain why my masters are able to use metal rasps to file their front teeth to sharp points. Perhaps they are impervious to pain. I wouldn't be surprised.

Did you know that most cats hate aluminum foil? I came across that while I was looking up the tooth thing.

Supposedly, if you want to keep the cat off your kitchen counter or clean laundry or whatever, you just need to put down some aluminum foil. They apparently don't like walking on it.

I'll have to test that out on my cat. It might help even the odds in the struggle for control of my home.

Explaining Painful Paper Cuts
July 17, 2003

Further proof that the heat must be getting to you guys: I just got a note from a bunch of people who are arguing about what would happen if you dammed up the Bay of Fundy, which is the spot with the world's greatest variations in tides.

They want to know if this would cause "enough of a variation to disturb the equilibrium between the Earth and the moon (and) cause the moon to eventually spiral into the Earth."

I have also received from a reader directions for a number of extremely nasty-sounding experiments you can do with a microwave, directions that I have no intention of passing along. You might hurt yourselves.

C'mon, folks, breathe. Flap your arms. Move around a bit. I think maybe you're not getting enough oxygen. OK? Do you feel better now?

Good. Now let's consider today's question:

Why does a paper cut hurt so much? Shouldn't it hurt less because it's a "cleaner" cut? Is it fibers from the paper that make it hurt more?

This turned out to be a lot more interesting than I expected. I found a number of explanations.

One is that it's mostly in your head. If you are chopping shallots in yet another attempt to make a decent bearnaise sauce and you cut your finger in the process, it might hurt, but you are not going to be especially surprised because, after all, you were handling a knife. Mr. Paper, on the other hand, is your friend. You do not expect a seemingly harmless sheet of paper to inflict a wound. The surprise — or maybe a sense of betrayal — makes the cut seem to hurt more.

Here's a more likely explanation: Your hands and fingers are jammed full of sensory nerve endings. Those endings are very close to the surface of the skin, just waiting to get sliced by a sharp piece of paper, at which time they will send a message to your brain that that it really, really hurts.

And then there is this: The edge of a sheet of paper may be sharp enough to cut you, but it's not exactly a razor. A dull cutting edge can do more damage than a sharp one because it makes a lot of little rips and tears.

Last, the questioner is correct about the fiber thing. As soon as you get cut, your body gets busy closing the wound, and it's possible some tiny particles of dirt or fiber are going to get sealed up in there, irritating all those nerve endings.

Purpose Of Hiccups A Mystery
July 24, 2003

No, Mr. Rogers was not an ex-Navy Seal who fought in Vietnam and had to wear long sleeves to cover up the tattoos on his arms. He was a Presbyterian minister, for Pete's sake.

I just don't know where you guys get these ideas or what comes over you.

Now settle down and pay attention to today's question.

Hiccups are annoying and irritating. So what's the point? Just what are they good for and why do we get them?

I didn't know this. I thought hiccups had some useful role in the scheme of things. It turns out nobody knows for sure what they're for. They're just like my masters. Their purpose in life is a mystery.

A hiccup, the medical word is *singultus*, is a contraction of some of your breathing muscles. Just as your breathing-in muscles start to move, the glottis — the opening between the vocal cords in your larynx — snaps shut, closing off your windpipe and making that "hic" sound. The Russian word for hiccup, by the way, is *ikota*.

Hiccups are associated with low levels of carbon dioxide in your bloodstream, which is why holding your breath sometimes makes them go away.

As noted, nobody knows for sure what the point of hiccups is, but there are some theories.

For one thing, babies in the womb start hiccuping around eight weeks, even before their breathing apparatus is working. One idea is that they hiccup to keep amniotic fluid from getting in their lungs, but that doesn't make much sense. Why use a breathing-in action for that purpose instead of breathing-out or coughing action?

The latest theory about hiccups comes from France, where some researchers have suggested we learned to hiccup about 370 million years ago, when some of our evolutionary ancestors started crawling out of the ocean into the fresh air.

They came up with this idea by studying primitive air-breathers such as lungfish and some amphibians with gills. Such animals get air by pushing water through their mouths and across their gills with the glottis closed to keep water out of the lungs. "Sacre bleu," the French researchers may have said, "That's a lot like hiccuping."

So why did hiccuping hang on in humans?

It's possible, some researchers think, that mammals adapted hiccuping as a means of teaching the young to nurse because suckling involves closing the glottis to keep milk out of the lungs.

Or maybe God just wanted to annoy us.

Hairy Tales In Time For Halloween
October 23, 2003

I was reading some ghost stories to my children the other night to get them in the mood for Halloween and, to make a long story short, in one of the stories a man's hair turned white from fright after spending the night in a haunted house. We are wondering if that could really happen.

You have to get your kids in the mood for Halloween? I thought kids were always in the mood for Halloween, like even in March. I like Halloween a lot, mostly because one of my little sweet patooties was born on Halloween. That was a pretty good day.

But I digress.

There have been many anecdotal accounts of people's hair turning white overnight, like the night before they were supposed to be executed or after receiving some great shock or being trapped in an elevator with one of my masters. Nobody seems to be quite sure how many of those stories are true.

Fortunately for you, I haven't thrown away my September 1981 copy of the *Archives of Dermatology*, which includes an article by J.D. Guin, V. Kumar and B.H. Petersen with the catchy title of "Immunofluorescence Findings in Rapid Whitening of Scalp Hair."

Unfortunately for you, I couldn't understand a word of it. Immunofluorescence? Yeah, like I'm really sure.

Anyway, this is what doctors think might be going on with the white-hair thing. It isn't so much that the whole head of hair suddenly turns white just like that. It's that a bunch of it falls out.

You know how some people have salt-and-pepper hair, a mixture of white or gray hair and darker hairs? I think that looks kind of cool, by the way.

Anyway, sometimes people with salt-and-pepper hair can be afflicted with a hard-to-spell condition called alopecia areata. Don't ask me what that means. I don't know.

However, if you have salt-and-pepper hair and you are suddenly smitten by this alopecia areata stuff, what happens is that your pepper hair, the pigmented hair, falls right off your head but the white or gray hair doesn't. Again, don't ask me why the white or gray hair doesn't fall out. It just doesn't, OK?

So it's not that all your hair turned white. It's just that the non-white hair fell out and you only have white or gray hair left.

Usually this happens over a certain period of time, like a few months or something. But apparently it is also possible for alopecia areata to be triggered by a sudden shock, such as finding out you're about to be executed or getting the bejabbers scared out of you.

Or by your mom reading you scary ghost stories just before you go to bed.

Flu Likes To Crash The Party
November 26, 2003

How does the flu get here every year? Is it something that grows in the ground, or does it travel on the air from many miles away?

Something that grows in the ground? I know I probably say this more than I should, but I just don't know what would become of you people if I weren't here to clear things up. Something that grows in the ground. Good Lord.

Did you get a flu shot yet? You should because they say this year's flu is supposed to be especially nasty. They were offering flu shots here at the Dark Tower, but I got mine someplace else. Like I trust my masters to inject me with something. Shaa.

The flu is a virus. Basically, it is a little packet of genes looking for someplace to move in and reproduce and generally whoop it up at your expense.

The flu also is very creative. It can mutate itself into a new variety on a pretty regular basis. That's why you need to get a new flu shot every year. It's not so much that the last one wore off. It's that the flu virus found a new way to get around the last shot so it can go on wearing party hats and singing and dancing and shacking up at your place.

As to your question: How does it get here every year? Because every year, you go to the opera and sit next to someone who is sneezing and coughing and waving tissues around and wearing a big frou-frou dress the size of a circus tent and complaining to her seatmate that she thinks she's coming down with something, and the next thing you know you feel like death warmed over.

In other words, the flu is spread by coughing and sneezing and shaking hands and so on and so forth.

And with travel so easy, it doesn't take very long for a particular strain of the bug to spread around the globe.

Furthermore, your chances of getting the flu are better in the winter, or at least when the weather is colder. That's because in the winter, you tend to be inside more and, hence, around other people more, and those other people are coughing and sneezing and shaking hands and wearing big frou-frou dresses and generally just broadcasting flu stuff around left and right.

Also, during colder weather, you are more likely to be inhaling dry, heated air that dries out your mucous membranes and, thus, makes your schnozz a more hospitable host for flu bugs wearing party hats.

So my advice would be that you should still go to the opera, but just don't sit next to anybody. Better yet, maybe you should just wait out in the car.

What's With All the Flakes?
December 10, 2003

Now I have a note from a kid — no doubt a sweet child but still... — who wants me to start a column on a certain date this month by wishing her chemistry teacher a Merry Christmas from her and her fellow students.

The date requested for this happens to be the date of a big chemistry exam. I guess the kid thinks if she pulled this off, somehow the chemistry exam might go easier.

You people. You people and your children. What am I going to do with you? Is it any wonder that I spend long hours in my dimly lit cubicle with a cold cloth over my eyes?

And the Diamondbacks let Miguel Batista go. What's up with that? They dumped Batista. He wrote poetry, for Pete's sake. Isn't it worth it just to have a poetic pitcher on the staff, even if he wasn't exactly a superstar?

Geez.

I'm sorry. I'm just crabby today. I have such a headache. But Craig Counsell and Batista both? Geez.

Let's turn to today's question, shall we? It will help take my mind off things.

Let's see here...I have a note from a guy who said he once snorted cayenne pepper up his nose to relieve his sinus problems. OK. I wonder if he's related to the kid with the chemistry teacher request. I've got a note from someone who says a lot of people probably wonder, as he does, what other cities are on the same latitude as Phoenix. Okey-dokey.

Let's do this one:

I sometimes visit my cousin, who is bald, but I've noticed he has a dandruff shampoo in his shower. My question is: If you don't have hair, can you even have dandruff?

Batista. OK, so he isn't exactly Nolan Ryan. I still can't believe they let him go.

All right, all right, if you want to talk about dandruff, we'll talk about dandruff.

Here's the story: Your cousin may be bald as a cue ball, but hair doesn't have anything to do with real dandruff. It is your cousin's scalp that is involved here.

The fact of the matter is nobody seems to be sure what causes dandruff. That is, real dandruff that falls off your head like a snow shower. It is a surplus of dead skin cells from your scalp. Nothing to do with your hair.

It might be caused by an allergy or a bad combination of shampoos and conditioners or just by dry conditions or even by stress. Or it might be some kind of fungal thing, which I don't even want to think about.

In any event, yes, you can be bald and still have dandruff. Again, it's from your scalp and not your hair.

And, oh, what the hell. Merry Christmas, Ms. Drewnowski, even if the test isn't today.

How Sexes Navigate Through Life
January 10, 2004

I am much smarter than my husband, and he's even smart enough to admit that. Why is it then that whenever we travel to a strange city or a new part of town this man, who can't even keep his children's names straight, always seems to know where everything is? Could he be an idiot savant about navigation?

An idiot savant? C'mon, lady, that's a bit much, don't you think? Give the guy a break.

The fact is men and women and apparently male and female rats and some other animals use different parts of their brains to navigate in a new environment.

We know this because researchers in Ulm, Germany did a test in which they wired up the brains of 12 men and 12 women and timed how long it took them to make their way through a virtual reality maze.

I think it may be nice to live in Ulm because it is a fun word to say and its name is nice and short so it would be easy to remember.

Anyway, the men finished the maze with average times about one minute faster than the women's times, and the researchers think it may have something to do with the fact that women tend to concentrate on their immediate surroundings while men take a broader view of the scene. So a woman may say, "Turn left at the green house and then right at the grocery store," while a man would wave vaguely at the horizon and say, "I'm pretty sure it's over there."

The brain scans showed that both men and women used the right hippocampus, which is a thing deep in your brain that is shaped like a banana. It's not actually the size of a banana, of course.

So both sexes used the right hippocampus, but only men also used their left hippocampus, while women supplemented their hippocampus work by also using their right prefrontal cortex, which is in the outer layer of your brain.

They think the right prefrontal cortex may be involved in helping women remember landmarks, while the extra hippocampus work by men may help with the more geometric, it's-over-that-way kind of thinking.

This is interesting: Some studies have shown changes in the structure of the left hippocampus of London taxi drivers, who have a pretty complicated job.

None of these differences in the way men or women navigate necessarily mean one sex is smarter than the other.

I'll leave that for you guys to work out among yourselves on a case-by-case basis.

Exploring Benefits Of Kissing
February 6, 2004

I have been shopping for a week or so for a used car for the second kid. This is not something I enjoy, but I have hit on a pretty crafty strategy for handling the process.

I simply walk up to the used-car salesperson, hold out a large wad of cash and say, "Take the money and just shoot me."

This way everyone is happy: The salesperson makes money, I don't ever have to go car shopping again, and the kid can buy a car herself with the insurance money.

So far this plan hasn't proved successful, but I'm still working on it.

Meanwhile, I have some alarming news in the form of today's question.

Is it true that you can burn 20 calories if you kiss for over a minute? If you could find this out, we would appreciate it. Thanks.

The alarming part of this is that the note was signed "the teenagers." Do you think that means all of them? They might be ganging up on us. That would make for a fearsome threat, wouldn't it? I think we need to try to keep them distracted, perhaps with kissing.

Did you know that kissing, in addition to being fun, is good for your teeth? According to some guy from the British Dental Association, after you eat your mouth is full of a sugary solution and a lot of acidic saliva, which causes plaque to build up. Kissing stimulates the flow of saliva and brings down plaque levels. I wonder if that's true.

Kissing also supposedly helps tone your cheek and jaw muscles and reduces stress, although a lot of the girls I've ever tried to kiss seemed to be a bit on the tetchy side.

Anyway, about the calories thing. I found a lot of different estimates of this, including one from the 1991 Kinsey Institute New Report on Sex, which said a real-good smackeroo burns 6.4 calories per minute of smackeroo-ing, compared with 11.2 calories burned per minute of jogging on a treadmill.

So that's about 384 calories per hour. Now, if you have to burn 3,000 calories to lose one pound, I'm thinking you need to kiss for almost eight hours before you had anything to show for it, other than really sore lips. That's a considerable amount of kissing.

On the other hand, if you took "the teenagers" and divided them into four groups and had each group jog off in a different direction for 24 hours straight, rest for a day and then jog back home, I calculate they each would burn up something like 32,400 calories, and the rest of us would get three days of peace and quiet. It's something to think about at least.

Scratching That Song That Stuck

April 27, 2004

One of you just sent me a picture of a "painting" that a friend made by using dryer lint of various colors.

Sigh.

You know, if I weren't so lazy and could get my masters to go along with it, and I doubt they would, I would organize a Valley 101 arts-and-crafts contest. Duct tape, dryer lint, carpet scraps, that sort of stuff.

That might be fun.

On second thought, it might be more scary than fun. I'll think of something else. Meanwhile, we shall take up today's question.

Every once in a while, I will get a song hung up in my brain that plays over and over and seems to never go away. It might even be one that I haven't heard recently. What causes this? Is it just my brain, or do others have the same experience?

You poor guy. I hope it's not that one Limp Bizkit song, which I am not going to name here for fear that it might get stuck in my brain.

Anyway, of course it's not just you. It happens to almost everyone.

Some research claims the "stuck song syndrome" happens to something like 97 percent of the American population. Why it happens is a little tricky to explain.

A few years ago a researcher at the University of Cincinnati named James Kellaris did a study of this insidious syndrome.

He determined that certain kinds of music create a "cognitive itch," what the Germans call an *ohrwurm*, or earworm.

"The only way to 'scratch' a cognitive itch is to rehearse the responsible tune mentally. The process may start involuntarily, as the brain detects an incongruity or something 'exceptional' in the musical stimulus.

"The ensuing mental repetition may exacerbate the 'itch,' such that the mental rehearsal becomes largely involuntary, and the individual feels trapped in a cycle or feedback loop," Kellaris said.

The tunes most likely to drive you nuts are repetitive and musically simple. (Try very hard right now not to think of "It's a Small World After All.")

And they have some unexpected twist to them, such as an irregular time or some unexpected notes.

You can read more about this at www.uc.edu/news/kellaris.htm.

But I'm warning you right now, the site includes some examples of highly stickable songs, so enter at your own risk.

Meanwhile, don't worry. Be happy.

Weather and stuff that makes my brain hurt...

Now we come to the weather section, weather and science sort of stuff. I have a great soft spot for the weather stuff especially. I guess that's why this is really my very favorite part of this book.

Some of you may recall that Valley 101 really got its start as a seven-day-a-week column mostly about weather. The first plan was that it was going to be mostly about outdoor recreation and a little bit about weather, but that didn't last long. There were two reasons for that.

First, I didn't particularly want it to be about outdoor recreation — hiking and stuff — even if my masters did. One day one of them suggested I go horseback riding. For what I get paid, I'm going to deal with a horse? Shaa. Horses have whacking great teeth and whacking great feet and weigh many pounds, if not tons. I prefer my swivel chair.

Secondly, the column made its seven-day-a-week debut at the very same time my masters redesigned the weather page — all the maps and charts and lists and so forth. And the column ran right next to all the newly redesigned weather maps and charts and lists and so forth. And people hated it. Not the column. They hated the new maps and charts and lists and so on.

And they assumed that because the column appeared right next to all the newly redesigned weather maps, etc., that I had something to do with it. So they called me to complain about it and they wrote to me to complain about it, which gave me a great opportunity to not write about hiking and horseback riding and so forth and instead to write about the weather maps, etc., and about how much people hated them and to say horrible, snarky things about my masters. It even led to the world famous great big Valley 101 journey to Fort Wayne, Ind., which is another story and one I'd just as soon forget about, if it's all the same to you. It was cold there.

As for the science stuff, it's OK, I guess. I don't have a real solid background in science. My high school biology and chemistry teacher spent all his time trying to disprove evolution and anything Niels Bohr ever wrote. Really. It had something to do with gingko trees. Or at least the evolution part did. I never did figure out what was going on with Niels Bohr. Then in college I landed in a science class for liberal arts majors that involved sitting around reading Time-Life books about frogs or whatever. So I don't know how much stock you want to put in the science parts. Most of them just confused me, and they still do.

Let's Stick To Mercury Over Foxes
January 10, 2001

Why do they use mercury in barometers and not some other fluid?

Hmm, that's a pretty good question. It's just goofy enough to be interesting and still not so hard that I had to miss Sally Jessy Raphael (Uncensored Home Videos!).

OK, let's start at the beginning. A barometer measures the pressure exerted on Earth by the weight of the atmosphere. Changes in atmospheric pressure help shape the weather. If you took a barometer to outer space you would be a dope because there is no atmosphere in the vacuum of outer space and you and the barometer would explode.

Anyway, most barometers measure atmospheric pressure by marking the rise or fall of a fluid in a glass column. You could make a barometer at home with a glass pop bottle, some colored water and a plastic straw and some modeling clay to seal the mouth of the bottle, but unless you were about nine years old you'd probably feel a little silly doing this.

Actually, you could use any fluid in a barometer. You could use red fox urine. But that would probably smell bad and would only serve to reopen that whole nasty business about whether red fox urine keeps rabbits away from your flower beds, and I don't want to go down that road again.

The reason they use mercury is because mercury is the heaviest liquid. A lighter fluid would require a taller column to measure the rise and fall of the air pressure. That's kind of interesting, huh? Water, according to the Web site where I looked this up, would require a column 30 feet tall to accurately gauge pressure changes. Mercury, because it is so heavy, needs a column only about 3 feet tall. Not all barometers use fluids. An aneroid barometer is based on springs that contract or expand depending on the pressure. Aneroid is from the Greek and means "no fluids," especially not red fox urine.

Wondering Where The White Goes
February 14, 2001

It turns out a number of you really do want to know where the white goes when snow melts.

I think this is just about the silliest question I ever heard, but after I said the other day I didn't know the answer and wasn't about to look it up, many of you wrote or called to press the issue.

A few of you even suggested that I was too lazy or spent too much time goofing off to do the research. Just for that I am not going to tell you the address of this extremely cool cow-catapulting game I just found on the Web. My personal best so far is 320 points and it's not even lunch-time yet. A pretty productive morning, I thought.

However, my masters put out a memo the other day saying they want the stories on the front page to have more impact and be more hard-hitting and stuff like that, so I figure if I'm ever going to crack A1 I'd better impact something or do some hard-hitting research.

So: *Where does the white go?*

That's just silly. It doesn't go anywhere, does it? It just isn't there, OK?

The real hard-hitting and impacting question here is this: If water is clear or opaque, and snow is frozen water, why is snow white?

OK, light comes in a whole rainbow of colors, right? The color of things is determined by which wavelengths of the spectrum they absorb or don't absorb.

A bunch of snow is made up of about a bazillion gazillion ice crystals. When light particles hit an ice crystal they get all scattered and bounced on to the next crystal, which also scatters and bounces them. After the light particles get scattered and bounced about a bazillion gazillion times by all those crystals, they just bounce right back out of the snow without any one band of color being absorbed. And all the bands of color together are white. So snow is white.

Coming tomorrow: Stand by to be hit hard and impacted by even more hard-hitting impact.

Walking Vs. Running In The Rain
February 20, 2001

If you are caught in the rain, moving from point A to point B, will you get wetter if you run or walk?

I don't know which is odder: The fact that I have received this question in one form or another at least three or four times in the past week or the fact that when I researched it I found five or six serious scientific studies of the matter.

One way or another, a lot of people have a lot of time on their hands.

Before I did any serious research, I posed the question to several of my colleagues around the newsroom, hoping one of them would come up with a plausible answer and thus spare me doing any actual work. All I can say is that it's a good thing some of these people have steady jobs in journalism because they might starve to death in the real world.

Anyway, I don't see what difference it makes. Wet is wet and unless point A and point B are just a few yards away, you're going to end up just as soaked if you run or walk.

But that's not the answer. The real answer, which involves stuff like kinematics, and relative velocity and vector components and something called flux, is:

dq/dVp = -p*x*At*Vr/(Vp {circ} 2)

Do you have any idea what that means? I sure don't.

I do understand this, however: In 1997 two meteorologists from the National Climatic Data Center in North Carolina waited for a rainy day, put plastic bags over their clothes and then donned identical sweat suits over the plastic bags. Then one ran and one walked 100 meters through the rain. Then they weighed their soggy sweat suits and determined the man who ran had absorbed 40 percent less water than the man who walked.

So there: The answer is you stay drier running.

Personally, I think you'd be better off carrying an umbrella, but what do I know? The kinematics of my relative velocity has flux all over it.

The Facts On Aridity, Humidity
April 13, 2001

The other day when it was raining, it made me wonder about this: Is it possible to have more than 100 percent humidity or less than zero percent? My husband thinks I am odd.

He may be right. I don't know. If he is just basing that on your question, you probably aren't all that odd, but there may be other factors involved, such as manner of dress, eating habits or the like.

First of all, no, it is not possible to have less than zero percent humidity. It's possible to have zero percent, but not less.

Ergo, hence and ipso facto, it would also seem to be impossible to have more than 100 percent relative humidity, but it turns out that's not true. This I learned from Randy Cerveny, an associate professor of geography at Arizona State University and the King of the Weather Wonks.

It turns out that you can have more than 100 percent relative humidity, although it is very rare.

According to Cerveny, it is called "supersaturation" and occurs in very cold conditions.

"The amount of water you can have in the air is a function of temperature. That's the whole concept of relative humidity — the relative is the temperature," he said.

Cold air can't hold as much water vapor as warm air. At 5 degrees Fahrenheit, a cubic yard of air is saturated by 0.07 cubic inches of water. At 68 degrees, that same amount of air and water has a relative humidity of 9 percent. I looked it up.

For supersaturation, you need temperatures of 30 or 40 below zero and very small water particles, so small as to be submicroscopic.

Under those conditions, the particles might be so small that they exist in the air without leaking out as moisture. If there are enough of them packed in there, the relative humidity can exceed 100 percent.

Does this make sense to you? Me neither, but that's what the man said.

Full Moon Insomnia? Beats Me
June 14, 2001

I am usually a very sound sleeper, but I always have trouble sleeping when the moon is full. Why?

I have a feeling I'm going to regret this one. Wouldn't you rather know why, if clouds are so big and heavy and full of moisture, they are not pulled to the ground by gravity? Now that's a good question. It's because rising drafts of air keep them floating.

The trouble with your question is that people believe all sorts of stuff about the full moon, and no matter what I write I'm going to be hearing for weeks after this from people who think the full moon has something to do with their dogs' psoriasis and people who believe that if you look at a full moon through a crystal while humming "Amazing Grace" you will get in touch with the mystical Eastern secrets of making money at home by stuffing envelopes. I actually did some real research on this, and there are a lot of people out there who say they have full-moon insomnia. Any number of explanations are offered.

Some people believe that if you are wakeful at night you are more likely to notice a full moon than a lesser moon and hence you connect sleeplessness with the full moon.

One piece I read said that under a full moon dust mites slow down but belted sandfish are more sexually active.

Some people say it has something to do with the gravitational pull of the moon. This supposedly upsets your body's rhythms or something. I suppose if the full moon can affect tides it could mess with your body parts, too. I don't know.

Some people think it is an evolutionary thing, a leftover from when we lived in trees or whatever and were more likely to be eaten by saber-toothed tigers on a moonlit night than on a dark night.

Then there's that whole werewolf thing, but I'm not even going near that.

In short, I don't know. Don't worry about it. Think about belted sandfish.

It's Curtains For Theory Of Bernoulli
October 12, 2001

Why does my shower curtain blow in toward the water instead of out when I turn the water on really high?

Doesn't anybody have any weather questions? Especially easy weather questions?

I thought this one was going to be hard, but it turned out people have actually made studies of this shower-curtain thing. And it turned out to be semi-interesting. I found this answer by David Schmidt, an assistant professor of engineering at the University of Massachusetts-Amherst, in a recent issue of the *Scientific American.*

According to Schmidt, most people used to think the shower-curtain thing was caused by the Bernoulli Effect. Can you believe it? The fools.

The Bernoulli Effect, of course, explains how an airplane's wings create lift, and holds that as a fluid accelerates, the pressure drops. Frankly, I don't see what that has to do with the shower curtain, but that's what the man said.

Another theory, the buoyancy theory, suggested that the hot water heated the air in the shower, thus reducing its density, and the curtain moved toward the lower pressure.

The problem with that is, the same thing happens whether the shower water is hot or cold.

Schmidt apparently set up a computer model using "modern fluid-simulation technology" to answer the question. Things must be kind of slow around the University of Massachusetts-Amherst.

OK, pay attention now: This is what Schmidt says. When the shower is running there is a certain amount of aerodynamic drag between the air and the water, and that drag imparts motion to the air and slows the droplets. The spray of the water creates a vortex that rotates around an axis that is perpendicular to the shower curtain. And the center of the vortex is an area of low pressure, like the center of a tornado. The pull generated by this low pressure is slight, but it is enough to suck a light, thin shower curtain toward it.

Metric Time Exists, But Who Cares?

November 1, 2001

If there are metric systems for measuring length and weight and so on, why isn't there a metric system for time?

Actually, there is. A number of people have put forward varying ideas for a metric time system.

I am not quite sure who these people are, but I suspect you would not want to find yourself sitting next to any of them on a long bus ride.

I studied several of these metric time proposals until my brain hurt and still cannot think what in the world got into these people.

Basically, a metric day would be the time required for the Earth to make one spin on its axis, divided into 25 hours. Some people might like the idea of an extra hour in the day, but they probably have never spent time with my masters.

The 25 hours would be divided in 100 metric minutes, which would be divided into 100 metric seconds. A metric hour would equal 57.6 real minutes.

A metric year would have 13 months with 28 days each, four weeks per month, seven days per week. Or it might have 12 months of 30 days, eight days a week and 3.75 weeks per month. The year would begin with the winter solstice.

I suppose there might be a good use for this, but I can't think of it offhand. Personally, I'd rather see a time system based on pie.

Speaking of time, a number of you have called or written to say your calendars or almanacs show the full moon falling today and not on Wednesday, as I said earlier this week. Many of you added that I am a nincompoop.

According to the U.S. Naval Observatory, the moon was as full as it's going to get this time around at 5:41 a.m. today Greenwich Mean Time, which was 10:41 p.m. Wednesday in Arizona.

And, yes, it was a blue moon, the second full moon in October. The phrase "blue moon" was first used to describe a rare or absurd event.

And I forgive you for doubting me.

This Dozen Thing Really Gets Gross
November 2, 2001

Why do so many things come by the dozen, like eggs?

Some guy called me up the other day and asked me this question, and when I said I didn't know, he promptly told me the answer.

If he already had an answer, I don't know why he bothered calling to ask me. Maybe he just wanted to play "stump the newspaper guy." I am perfectly capable of playing that by myself.

Anyway, this guy said it has to do with the number of joints in the fingers of one hand. Let's say you are sorting a big pile of turnips into smaller piles. And you can't count very well. If you could count you could get a better job than sorting turnips, which cannot be a very exciting career.

So, you move the turnips with one hand and with the other hand, palm up, you tick off the joints of your fingers with your thumb. When you go through the 12 joints, you start another pile of turnips. Hence, stuff got packaged by 12s.

I don't know if this is true. It sounds reasonable. Or maybe it has something to do with 12 months in a year or the 12 apostles or the fact that it takes Jupiter 12 years to orbit the sun. I spent a lot of time trying to track it down without much success.

I did find out that both the United States and Great Britain have "dozenal" organizations. The goal of the Dozenal Society of America, according to its Web page, is "the conduct of research and education of the public in the use of Base Twelve in numeration, mathematics, weights and measures, and other branches of pure and applied science."

You've got to figure that this is a real fun bunch. I wonder what its annual conventions are like.

While we are on the subject, the word "gross," meaning a dozen dozen, comes from the Latin *grossus*, meaning thick or large. Grocer comes from the same source and originally meant someone who sold wholesale or in very large lots, such as a gross of turnips.

Brrr. Why It's So Cold At Sunrise

December 6, 2001

Why does it feel colder when I take my son to school at 7:30 a.m., when the sun is shining, than it does when I take my walk in the dark two hours earlier?

Because it is. This, of course, does not make sense, but there you have it.

For example, take Monday, a nice, clear day. At 4 a.m., the temperature at Sky Harbor was 52. At 5 a.m., it was 50. At 8 a.m., it was 49, and at 9 a.m., it was 53.

This has to do with something called blackbody radiation, which has to do with physics and is only going to make your brain hurt if I try to explain it. Take my word for it. David Runyan, a National Weather Service meteorologist, explained this to me.

Sunlight is shortwave radiation. It does not significantly heat up the atmosphere as it passes through. What it does heat up is the soil and buildings and your steering wheel. Those things in turn give off heat in long-wave radiation. That's what warms the air.

It just takes a while for all this to happen, for the Earth to warm up and cool off. That's why the hottest part of the day is usually late in the afternoon and not at noon when the sun is directly overhead. And why the coldest part of the day is just about the time the sun rises.

We'll Shed No Tears For Rain Drops
January 13, 2001

I know snowflakes are six-sided crystals. What shape are raindrops?

What shape are raindrops? What kind of question is that? You people never cease to amaze me. You know, my horoscope Friday said, "If you can avoid going to work, do so." I should have listened.

Wouldn't you rather know about butterflies? Did you know the Arizona Federation of Garden Clubs is asking the Legislature to name the two-tailed swallowtail the official Arizona state butterfly? I don't know why we need an official state butterfly, but I suppose there's no harm in it, and it will give the Legislature something to do. Maybe they'll offer a tax rebate to people who convert their back yards into alternate butterfly environments.

Anyway, the raindrop thing turned out to be kind of interesting, in a weather-wonkish sort of way. I always thought raindrops were supposed to look sort of like a teardrop, pointy on the top and round on the bottom. This, like so much of the stuff I always thought, turned out to be wrong.

Raindrops start off round, like little marbles. They can be any-where from 0.01 inch to one-quarter inch in size. That's pretty big. I wonder what would happen if a quarter-inch raindrop hit a two-tailed swallowtail butterfly right on the head.

So, a raindrop starts off round, but as it falls, the air pressure flat-tens out its bottom. The sides of the drop bulge out because the pressure on the sides is lower. So it ends up looking more kind of mound-shaped than teardrop-shaped. If it gets to be bigger than a quarter-inch, it splits in two little round drops and the process starts again.

While we're on the subject, the reason snow crystals are six-sided is that that is the shape water molecules take when they freeze. It has to do with the way electrical attractions bind oxygen and hydrogen molecules.

Desert Story: Dew Point Can Be Minus

March 8, 2002

Many of you have called or written lately to inquire about the dew point readings, a topic usually reserved for the steamy days of summer.

Specifically, you are concerned, some of you to the point of near hysteria, about a recent spate of negative dew point readings. Soothe yourselves, meine Freunde. All will soon become clear; calm will be restored; and life will continue in all its fullness and wonder.

Let's review: The dew point temperature is the point at which water vapor in the air changes from a gas to water or a solid (dew or frost, depending on the temperature). It has to do with relative humidity and temperature and the fact that the amount of water the air can hold varies with the temperature. This, of course, will be of great concern in a few months when people crank up their evaporative coolers.

As good old David Runyan of the National Weather Service put it, the dew point is a "calculated" temperature as opposed to a "sensed" temperature.

I found a formula for calculating the dew point and, trust me, you don't want to hear about it. It ran for three full lines of type on an 8½ by 11 sheet of paper. You don't want to fool around with stuff like that, because under certain atmospheric conditions, it can make your brain explode.

So anyway, yes, it is possible to have a negative dew point, just as it is possible to have a temperature below zero. And that is just what has been happening. The air over the Valley has been so dry lately that humidity readings have fallen as low as 3 percent, and dew points have been as low as minus 9 degrees Fahrenheit.

So if the dew point is minus 9, that means the temperature would have to fall to 9 below zero before the air could not hold any more water and frost would form. Since cold air cannot hold as much water as warm air, that means it's pretty darn dry, which is why my firm yet somehow sensuous lips are all chapped, and my socks dry really fast on the clothesline.

Do Batteries Really Need To Be Chilled?

April 6, 2002

I had a call a little while ago from a guy who thinks someone should collect bellybutton lint from celebrities and movie stars and other famous people and use it to stuff a pillow and then auction the pillow for charity.

I worry about you people. A lot.

I also had a very nice note from a lady in British Columbia who went on about what a nice spring they are having there and then asked:

Does it extend the life of batteries if you store them in plastic bags in the fridge?

OK, let's all follow along now. Batteries produce electricity when the chemicals inside them react with each other and start throwing electrons around. This is known as a redox reaction.

In most common batteries, AA, AAA, C, D, the chemicals are usually zinc and manganese. When you throw the switch, the zinc passes electrons to the manganese, an electric current is created and your Walkman starts playing and you scream and yank the headphones off because your kid went off and left it with the volume on high.

Now, even when they are not in use batteries do leak a little bit of electricity, an infinitesimal amount, and that uses up an infinitesimal amount of the chemicals and thus shortens the life of the battery infinitesimally.

Infinitesimal is a pretty good word, don't you think? I would use it more often if it were easier to spell.

Chemical reactions take place more slowly at lower temperatures. So if you put the batteries in the fridge, you slow down the chemical reaction and thereby reduce the leakage.

It is the same as a car battery in bitter winter weather. The cold slows down the chemical reaction to the point that the battery won't turn over the engine. Bummer.

I think the practice of chilling batteries used to be more common. Modern alkaline batteries have such a long shelf life that chilling them doesn't seem necessary.

Smells Like At Least 110 (Degrees) To This Guy

June 28, 2002

Today's question:

My husband says he can tell the temperature by the way the air smells. He claims he can tell how hot it is within a few degrees just by sniffing the air. I've tried testing him, but I don't know how accurate our patio thermometer is.

He can tell the temperature by smell? It's too bad vaudeville is dead. He could have taken his act on the road.

Does he do any other tricks?

I am not sure what to make of this. Most of us, after we've lived here awhile, become fairly well attuned to even small changes in the temperature. Sometimes you can just sort of feel it.

A couple of years ago, a colleague correctly predicted the end of the monsoon by the quality of the early morning light.

But I never heard of anyone smelling the temperature.

This is not to say it might not be true. The weather can be pretty odiferous.

We can smell rain coming. We can smell ozone if lightning strikes close by.

And there is that distinctive smell of hot asphalt just after a light monsoon rain. I really hate that smell.

And when it's hot, there are more things to smell.

Higher temperatures mean more molecules are flying around and breaking loose from solids or liquids and becoming vapors that we can smell.

So if your husband says he can smell the temperature, maybe he can.

Stranger things have happened. Take my masters, for instance.

Laundry Physics Isn't Rocket Science

September 18, 2002

I mentioned today's question to a colleague, who urged me not to write about it. He said knowing the answer would take all the mystery out of doing his laundry.

I don't know what's so mysterious about doing the laundry. My whites go in one pile, colors in another and my lacy underthings in a third. All right, the lacy underthings are a bit mysterious, but other than that, it's pretty straightforward.

However, if your laundry day is one of mystery, shrouded in a happy cloud of unknowing, you might want to skip today's column.

Today's question:

My husband and I have asked this question to everyone we know and to no avail. How do those Downy fabric-softener balls work?

Aren't those things great? I love them. I wish I'd invented Downy balls. If I had invented Downy balls, I'd probably be rich by now and far away from the icy cold grasp of my masters and their cruel intentions.

Anyway, the answer comes from the February 2000 edition of *The Physics Teacher*, which, as you may have guessed, is a magazine for physics teachers. You've probably thrown that issue out by now.

And, best of all, it is so simple that even I understood it.

Downy balls work on Newton's First Law: "An object will move with a constant velocity (which may be zero) unless acted on by a net external force."

OK? Now consider the Downy ball in all it's beauty and ingenious design. It has a rubber seal that you pull tight after you put in the softener, and it has a rubber weight hanging down into the ball.

As the washer begins to spin, the ball is thrown against the hard wall of the drum. However, the rubber weight has momentum and still has room to move forward until it strikes the inside surface of the ball.

Eventually, the action of the weight tips the ball to a certain angle, pulling loose the plug. Water rushes in, and the liquid softener is dispensed.

As Newton himself would have said:

Bippity, boppity, boo.

Bubbling Over With Weird Stuff
December 11, 2002

Did you see that story the other day about the lobster someone caught off the coast of Nova Scotia? It was half albino and had both male and female lobster sex organs.

A half-albino hermaphrodite lobster. How creepy would that be? I'd rather be on an elevator with one of my masters than with a half-albino hermaphrodite lobster. Let's not think about it. It will keep you awake at night. Let's discuss something more pleasant. Christmas lights, perhaps.

How do bubble lights work?

Bubble lights. Gee, I hadn't thought about those in years. They were cool. Do you have some really old ones? People collect them. You could probably get some money for them if they still work.

Bubble lights were invented in the 1930s by a man named Carl Otis who worked for Montgomery Ward. They didn't get on the market until 1945, when they were sold by the National Outfit Manufacturers Association. They didn't really catch on until the 1950s, which is odd because at the time, they were the first real innovation in Christmas lights in a long time.

Bubble lights are pretty simple. A liquid is sealed in a glass tube and brought to boil by the heat of an enclosed light.

The liquid was generally methylene chloride, which has a very low boiling point of 104 degrees. That means you make the stuff boil just by holding it in your hands.

Some of the earlier versions used different types of oil, rapeseed or castor or cod liver oil.

And sometimes the manufacturers would put salt or sugar crystals in the tube. Neither of those dissolve in methylene chloride and they made things more bubbly, like putting salt in your beer, which is a disgusting habit.

As long as we are on the subject, and as long as there is still a ways to go to the end of this: The first guy to put electric lights on a Christmas tree was Edward Johnson, who was an associate of Thomas

Edison. This was in 1882, just three years after Edison figured out the light bulb.

There were 80 white, red and blue lights "in these dainty glass eggs," according to a newspaper account at the time, and the whole thing had a "picturesque and uncanny aspect."

The first electrically lit tree in the White House was in 1895, with Grover Cleveland at the switch. After that, they became quite fashionable and people would pay up to $2,000 in today's money to hire an electrician to set up their trees.

So, you can go to bed tonight grateful that you didn't need an electrician to do your tree and sleep soundly while visions of half-albino hermaphrodite lobsters dance in your head.

Know-It-All Teen Knows Nothing

January 13, 2003

Yesterday I opened the refrigerator door and the butter dish shot out onto the floor. My 18-year-old college student son picked all of the various pieces of butter off the floor, put them onto the dish and put it back in the refrigerator while he counted to five. He said that germs do not have time in five seconds to get on the butter or anything else that hits the floor. Is this true?

Let's review what we've learned so far, shall we?

Is this correct? You took advice from an 18-year-old male on food, food preparation, cleanliness, germs, or sanitation in general?

Madam, stay exactly where you are. Do not leave your home. For heaven's sakes, don't eat anything your son may have touched. Come to think of it, don't touch him, either. From headquarters here at the Dark Tower, a Valley 101 Emergency Response Team has been dispatched to your home to check your vital signs and give you a good talking-to.

I only hope it's not too late.

I don't know when the so-called Five Second Rule took effect, but I'd recommend peaceful civil disobedience for most of its clauses.

Consider this: If you drop, say, a pat of butter on the floor and if there are germs or bacteria or viruses or parasites or whatever on the floor, the pat of butter is going to be colonized by one or all of those critters whether it is on the floor for one second or one hour.

On the other hand, if you dropped, say, a dry cracker on a dry, reasonably clean floor, most likely you could retrieve it and eat it in relative safety.

I could not find any real hard and fast scientific information about the Five Second Rule, with the exception of a report on a science project by some kid in California who dropped dry and wet swabs on his kitchen floor and then checked them for creepy crawlies.

Bright kid. I hope he won a prize for this.

He found the average number of bacteria colonies on a dry swab was 56 after two seconds on the floor and 58 after five seconds.

However, on the wet swabs the average number of colonies was 281 after two seconds and too high to count after five seconds.

Too high to count. Euuuu.

I suppose you have to make allowances for what kind of floor you dropped the food on.

Maybe scooping up and eating a piece of popcorn you dropped on your nice, clean kitchen floor isn't going to kill you. On other hand, I doubt if you'd want that piece of popcorn you dropped on the floor at the movie theater.

Or at least, I hope you wouldn't.

The Yin And Yang Of Time
January 22, 2003

What is the opposite of time?
Umm...*Newsweek?*

Look, that's a pretty complicated question, and for 50 cents you aren't going to get a really deep and thoughtful answer. Even at the $2 Sunday rate you're not going to get much of an answer to a question like that. Which is not to say there is no answer. There's a bunch of them.

As usual with such weighty matters, I consulted with my pal Richard Jacob, who is professor emeritus of physics at Arizona State University, so you know he didn't just fall off the turnip truck.

He pondered mightily on this because pondering mightily is what professors emeritus do and then, knowing whom he was talking to, explained it in the simplest terms possible.

First of all, consider this: In this case, time is used as a noun. Can a noun have an opposite? Maybe so, but what is the opposite of, say, horse? Non-horse? Car? Non-car?

So if you define time as the phenomenon of events succeeding other events, then the opposite of time would be a state of timelessness in which no events succeed other events. Like my cubicle a few hours before quitting time. There sure aren't any events going on there.

Or you could argue that the opposite of time is space in the sense that they complement each other, sort of a yin and yang thing or male and female or good and bad.

That's a pretty good answer, if you think about it, although I have no intention of thinking about it for very long because I'm pretty sure that, if I did, my brain would start to hurt. It's aching a bit as it is.

Or there is an even more complicated answer: the concept of reverse time.

If you knock a priceless crystal vase off a shelf, it will fall to the floor and shatter, and its owner will never invite you over again. There is no way under the laws of the natural world that you can reverse the fall of the vase. However, Jacob said, there are specific laws of physics that operate the same in either time or reverse time. Think of a billiard ball as moving forward in time when you hit it from point A to point B. If you then hit it just so from the opposite side with the same force, it would follow the same path from B to A, only in reverse. Kind of the same thing happens in physics with subatomic particles and stuff. If time is a variable, they react the same way in time or reverse time. Or at least that's what Jacob said.

Time Flies When You Are Aging
June 3, 2003

Why does time seem to go by faster the older I get?

Hey, tell me about it. Since when is it June? It was just March the other day. For that matter, since when is it 2003? And what in the world happened to my little girls?

The thing of it is, is that you are not imagining this. Time really does go by faster as you get older. That bites, if you ask me, but it can't be helped.

People have been wondering about this for years. William James, who is more or less the father of modern psychology, wrote about it in 1890 in *The Principles of Psychology*, which is more or less the father of modern psychology books.

Basically, you have to start with the Aristotelian idea that time exists only in your mind as a way of measuring or understanding change. OK?

You measure time in terms of the total time in your memory. If you are 5 years old, one year is a whole 20 percent of your life. If you're 25, that same year is just one-twenty-fifth of your life. If you're 50, it's one-fiftieth, or a mere 2 percent, of your life. No wonder things seem to be zipping along so fast.

If you want the looooong explanation of this, you'll need to read an essay by James Kenney, an expert on microwave semiconductor measurements, titled "Logtime: The Subjective Scale of Life — the Logarithmic Time Perception Hypotheses."

I'm sorry, but the title alone is enough to make my brain hurt. In a nutshell, Kenney has come up with a way of measuring your perception of time on a logarithmic scale. Here's an excerpt from a part I actually understood:

"The older we become, the faster we seem to age or, conversely, the shorter the years seem to be. Mathematically, this relationship is said to be either logarithmic or exponential, depending on which variable is used as the reference: The length of the years seems to shrink logarithmically if we regard our subjective aging as uniform, while the speed of passage of these years seems to increase exponentially if we regard the years as being of equal length."

Kenney's ideas run along the same lines as the "Weber-Fetcher law" for perception of physical stimuli.

Don't get your hopes up. For 50 cents, you are not getting an explanation of the Weber-Fetcher law.

So what's to be done?

You could spend some time with my masters. The minutes and hours just drag by, believe me.

However, a less grueling and more practical answer is to do what Kenney suggests: Ignore it. Time may be speeding up, but you can't stop it. Get out there and enjoy it while you can.

The Skinny On Dust Bunnies

January 6, 2004

What exactly are dust bunnies and what causes them? Our cat is afraid to go under the bed, and I looked and some of them seem to have mutated into what looks like a dust boa constrictor.

I thought this was kind of a dopey question at first, but then as the day wore on it started looking better and better, and when I actually started in on it, it turned out to be kind of interesting.

The dust that goes into breeding a healthy dust bunny is made up of little bits of your skin that flaked off and stuff that fell off your clothes or furniture and pieces of hair and pollen and tiny bits of plain old dirt.

So what makes all these things come together to form dust bunnies? It's our old friend, Mr. Electricity.

Things are made up of atoms, and in a healthy, well-nourished atom, things are in balance with the same number of electrons as protons.

When things get broken apart, such as dust, the electrons tend to sort of get loose and go wandering around and the electrical balance gets all out of whack. The next thing you know the electrons are hanging around with opposite charges, and the little bits of dust get attracted to and stuck on other little bits of dust, and pretty soon you've got a dust bunny on your hands, a dust bunny held together by static electricity.

And of course they tend to gather under the bed or some other place where there isn't much air movement to break them up.

The obvious solution is to get out the vacuum cleaner and thin out the herd a bit. Of course, in doing so you might also be sucking up some cosmic dust that traveled millions of miles through space to end up under your bed, but there is plenty of the stuff to go around, so don't worry about it.

The universe, it turns out, is a very dusty place. Every year tons and tons of cosmic dust land on Earth, and if that much hits such a small target in the vastness of space, think how much more of it there must be out there floating around.

Cosmic dust is the leftover from a supernova explosion or from some collision or other event way out in space. It is easy to tell the difference between space dust and plain old house dust, if you happen to have a spectroscope or some other sophisticated scientific devices in your closet.

For one thing, cosmic dust has a lot of nickel and iron in it. It also contains some of the same stuff that goes into forming your DNA, which means little bits of the stuff that make you are drifting around in space. That strikes me as kind of a nice idea, although I'm not sure why.

Glass Talk Gets Thick With Worry

January 26, 2004

A friend recently sent me one of those lists of odd or unusual "facts" that you find on the Web sometimes. One of the items said that the windows in some very old churches in Europe are thicker at the bottom than at the top because glass is a liquid and the glass in the windows had flowed down. Is this true?

Is what true? That glass is a liquid or that part about the windows?

The thing about the windows is hooey.

The windows in some medieval buildings are thicker at the bottom because of the process used to make them.

It's too complicated to go into here, and besides, why would you want to know about it anyway?

So you could build medieval windows?

The part about glass being a liquid or a solid is a little more complicated.

Obviously, if you rap on a pane of glass with your knuckles, it is a solid.

However, in theory it isn't a solid and it isn't quite a liquid, either.

In a liquid, the molecules are constantly bumping around, making and breaking loose connections.

In a solid, the molecules are locked together in very rigid orderly bonds.

In glass, the molecules don't do either of those things.

OK, now don't write or call to tell me about different forms of glass, like polystyrene, for example. For the purpose of this discussion, we're just going to discuss glass like the glass in your windows, OK?

So you make glass by mixing sand with some other stuff — soda ash, limestone, etc., depending on what you're making — and getting it really, really hot and then cooling it rapidly, super-cooling it to below its freezing point.

When you super-cool this mixture of molten sand, etc., its little molecules don't have time to arrange themselves as crystals, like in an ice cube. What happens is that the molecules move very, very slowly and the viscosity of the mixture gets thicker and thicker and finally the molecules pretty much just come to a halt and you have glass.

This is called an amorphous solid. The molecules stick together enough to give the glass some rigidity, but they do not stick together in an orderly manner, like in a real solid.

So if glass is really just an extremely viscous liquid, it would flow, and I guess it does. It just doesn't flow at the pace we can comprehend. One source I read said it would take 10 million years or more for the glass in a church window to flow downward to the point that the bottom of the window was 5 percent thicker than the top.

So don't worry about it.

Forecasts Don't Rain On My Parade

March 4, 2004

Sometimes I wonder if maybe I shouldn't try to make this column more topical. You know, make it more grown-up, more up-to-date. Maybe I could arrange to perform gay marriages in this space or take a serious, thoughtful stand on weasels or endorse someone for something. Something along those lines.

Then I think, "Nah, that would be too much work." So instead I'll stick with hard-hitting answers to hard-hitting questions such as:

Why are weather forecasts still so inaccurate? We often hear a storm "just snuck in" or a predicted storm "just fell apart." We're talking about storms here, big things many miles high and wide, driven by lows and highs that are hundreds of miles across, steered by huge jet streams that don't make sudden turns. We've got a bunch of the world's biggest computers, thousands of monitoring stations, hundreds of trained meteorologists, and multiple competing forecasting services. So why do they so often get things wrong?

Hey there, Mr. Grumpypants. What's eating you? We are living in paradise and in the very best time of the year in paradise, and I just got two nice shirts on sale, and you're all crabby. Gee whiz.

OK, sometimes the weather forecasts are not perfect, but then what is? If things — the weather, baked goods, elections, love — always turned out just as expected, what would be the fun of that?

And I think you have sort of answered your own question. The weather is miles high and miles wide with fronts and systems and temperatures and jet streams and all that other stuff going on. In other words, there are a gazillion variables involved, even in fairly short-term forecasts. And the variables aren't all great whopping big things. The forecast you hear or read for the Valley may not necessarily take into consideration that big asphalt parking lot down the street or a grassy park around the corner or just how the wind happens to hit your palm tree. All those things make a difference in your own personal weather.

And then there is the chaos factor, that business about how a butterfly flapping its wings in Rangoon could affect how much sunlight falls on a sleeping dog's rear end in Mesa.

If you actually kept track, I bet you'd find that forecasts, especially short-term outlooks, are pretty much accurate. So when the unexpected does happen, it seems even more unexpected and more like a big deal than it really is.

So take off those wingtips of crabbiness, buster, and put on the flip-flops of happiness. The weather, like life, is full of surprises. That's why it's so interesting.

Opera Far Superior To Numbers
March 13, 2004

Today's question is about physics. And possibly astronomy. Or it may be about algebra or something like that because there seem to be a lot of numbers involved and some "x's" and "to the xth powers" and stuff like that. I'm not really sure. I should have paid more attention in school.

(Important note to young readers: You know how you sit there in class — a class in whatever — and think to yourself, "Why do I have to learn about this stuff? I'm never going to need to use it." Take it from me, kids: You never know. On the other hand, if I had learned a lot of this stuff back then, I might have ended up in a real, grown-up job in which I couldn't sit at the kitchen table in my bathrobe and sing made-up lyrics to opera or Broadway musicals while I write this stuff. That's one especially nice thing about opera: Chances are, you can't understand the words anyway, so you can just sing whatever you want and sing it really loud. But you should hear me in *The Music Man*. I'm deadly in *The Music Man*, and I know the real words.)

But I digress. Here's the question:

I believe the speed of light is always the same. My boyfriend says it can change. Who is right?

Sorry, sweetie, but your boyfriend is right. This is not to say that your parents would approve of him, but he is correct on this point.

It is true that we always talk about things moving at the speed of light and light years and so on. Actually, I find this hardly ever comes up in conversation, but I bet there are people who always talk about things like that. And it is true that the speed of light is 186,000 miles per second or thereabouts.

However, that is 186,000 miles per second in a vacuum. When light passes through things, such as glass or air or water or between my masters' ears, it is slowed. The degree to which it slows is called the refractive index, and it depends on how dense the air or glass or whatever is.

Granted, it isn't slowed much. It's not like you're going to be getting a haircut, and the barber all of a sudden says, "Has the light slowed down a lot lately, or is it just me?" But yes, the speed of light can be changed.

In fact, last year some scientists at Harvard, working with some Russian colleagues, said they brought the speed of light to a dead halt by shooting it through rubidium gas, whatever that is.

I'm not sure they should fool around with stuff like that, and I could go into greater detail, but the second act of *Rigoletto* is coming up, and I'm on.

Running, Or Batting, Hot And Cold

April 14, 2004

Do you know what fulgurites are? Neither did I until somebody sent me a note about them after Monday's column about lightning.

A fulgurite is what you get when lightning strikes sand or a rock. The lightning superheats the sand or the rock and forms hollow tubes of stuff like glass. In sand, you can sometimes find them several feet under the surface. That would be something to come across, don't you think? I looked up some pictures of fulgurites. They're pretty cool.

Fulgurites, however, are not the topic at hand. The topic at hand is baseball and the weather.

Why do baseball announcers say that baseballs travel farther in warm air than in cold air? Doesn't warm air hold more water vapor than cold air, thus slowing the ball down?

You are correct. Warm air can hold more water vapor than can cold air. Let us ask ourselves why. Let us also ask ourselves why it is so hard to find really good coleslaw around here. No, let us ask ourselves that at another time and for now confine our thoughts to warm air and water vapor.

Warm air can hold more water vapor than cold air for the same reason that a baseball will travel farther in warm air than in cold: because it is less dense.

Let us say that you are at beautiful Wrigley Field in Chicago and you have two hypothetical at-bats against Kerry Wood and his 95 mph fastball, one on a hot day in June and one on a cold day in April. In which case will the batted ball travel farther?

The obvious answer is neither because if you are anything like me, the idea of standing in against Kerry Wood's 95 mph fastball would leave you curled up in a fetal position, whimpering softly and possibly even mewling.

However, if you were a real baseball player and hit both balls with equal force, the warm-weather ball would go farther, maybe even an extra 20 feet or so.

And, at equal temperatures, it also would go farther in the thin air of Denver than it would at sea level in San Diego.

As for humidity, that gets a little complicated. It doesn't seem like it would be so, but at equal temperatures, humid air actually is less dense than dry air so you should pick up a few feet on a humid day. However, the humidity also makes the ball itself slightly heavier and thus a little less lively, which would offset the air-density thing.

Stick A Fork In The Myth Of The Spoon

April 21, 2004

We recently had a visitor from Germany over to our house for dinner. In the course of the meal, we opened but did not finish a bottle of champagne. We were discussing how to keep the remaining champagne bubbly, and our guest said that in Germany they suspend a teaspoon in the neck of the bottle and that keeps it fresh. We tried it, and the next day the champagne was still bubbly. How does that work?

I just got an e-mail from a guy who recently moved to the Valley from Los Angeles and doesn't like the barbers here. He thinks Valley barbers are "uppity." That was the very word he used. Now, I don't know about you, but if I had just moved to paradise from Los Angeles, I don't believe I'd fuss much about barbers. Perhaps that's just me.

Anyway, about the spoon in the champagne thing: That was a new one to me, but as luck would have it, it didn't take me long to find the answer.

This is how it worked: It didn't. With all due respect to your guest from overseas, he was deluded. He was passing along an old frau's tale. As Pogo might have put it, the spoon trick was a fig newton of his imagination.

I found the answer to this one in the annals of *New Scientist*, which is a very useful and often quirky British magazine about, as you may have guessed, science.

I'd subscribe, but then I wouldn't be able to afford *Boys' Life*.

The scientists at *New Scientist* did what you and your friend from Germany didn't do — a controlled test. In other words, they suspended a spoon handle in one open bottle of champagne and let a second open bottle of the same champagne stand unspooned.

Then they did blind taste tests every few hours and asked tasters to rate the fizz factor of the two wines on a scale of 0 to 100.

It turned out that the bubbliness of both bottles declined at the same rate, and that neither was considered to be truly flat until they had been standing for about 96 hours. In other words, both bottles declined in fizz at the same rate.

The lesson here, according to *New Scientist*, is that champagne just doesn't go flat as quickly as most of us assume that it does.

And since most of us rarely have two bottles of bubbly standing open for hours at the same time, it is easy to imagine that the spoon trick worked, even if it didn't.

Feeling Flush With Insights Into Physics

May 15, 2004

You're in luck today. I was working on a fairly mundane column about the sex life of corn and was having a hard time thinking up vaguely dirty puns to fill it out and even I was getting bored with it.

Just when I was about to doze off, out of the blue another question came in that I thought was a lot more interesting, although it lacks the potential for semi-smutty jokes about the sex life of corn.

Plus, I found an answer to it, which is always helpful.

This is from some guy in Prescott Valley who claims his name is Jack and for all I know it may well be.

When the wind is blowing, I notice the water level in the toilet bowl seems to decrease. Why would that happen?

You know, I've been through Prescott Valley many times, but I never really stopped there. Maybe I should drop in the next time I'm up that way to see if they haven't got anything better to do than to watch the water level in the toilet bowl go up or down. I'm sure they do, but who knows? Like I said, I've never really visited there.

Anyway, I found the answer to this matter online in the form of a newsletter for physics teachers in Wisconsin.

I'd print the Web address, but it's one of those long, complicated ones with lots of odd characters in it, and I'd probably get it wrong anyway. If you're really interested, you can poke around a bit and find it yourself.

This is the deal: The water level in the bowl doesn't necessarily just drop, but it does bounce up and down.

Oscillate, that's the word.

And this is why, according to the physics teachers of Wisconsin: It's Bernoulli's principle, which has to do with the relationship between pressure and fluid velocity.

When wind blows across the top of the air vents for a septic system, it causes relatively low pressure, compared to the still air inside the vent.

Since fluid flows from high pressure to low pressure, air gets drawn up and out the vent, lowering the pressure in the vent. This turns the toilet bowl into a manometer, which I guess is a device for measuring the pressure of gas or liquid.

So the air pressure in your house is pushing against the water at one rate, and the air in the vent is pushing at another rate, which varies with the wind.

And, yes, for every kernel of corn, there is one corn silk.

Which reminds me: A kernel of corn walks into a bar and meets a silk and...

Assorted oddities...

Well, it looks like we've saved the best part for last — the miscellaneous stuff, odds and ends. This is really the most interesting section, or at least I think so. If I were you I'd just skip those other parts and only read this one. It's the best.

There are only so many weather questions you can answer day in and day out, and after a while the weather well began to run dry. Then people, under the delusion that I might know the actual answers, started sending in questions about just about anything.

Not too long ago I got a question from a guy who wanted to know this: If you could sit at a point just outside the edge of the expanding universe, what would happen to you when the universe got there? I'm not smart enough to know if this is the sort of question that would intrigue great minds like Newton or Einstein or Gabby Hayes, or if this guy was just stoned when he wondered about. Still, it's a pretty good question, don't you think?

It's a good question not because it might actually make sense or because there might actually be an answer to it. It's a good question because it is an example of just how amazing people are and just how amazing the things that people wonder about are.

If there is anything I have learned from doing Valley 101 it is how unfailingly odd and interesting and curious people are. It would never occur to me in 100 years to wonder what would happen if you were outside the universe and it suddenly caught up with you. But here's some guy, stoned or otherwise, who wants to know. Of course, I have no intention of trying to answer it. It sounds like a lot of work.

I get this stuff every day. What kind of animal is the neat that they use to make neat's-foot oil? Why do white pants make your butt look big? Can havoc be anything other than wreaked? Why don't tires come in any colors other than black and white? There's just no end to it and no end to how interesting people are.

I think maybe this one is my all-time favorite, or at least it is until I go in to the office tomorrow to see what's turned up next: What does the sun smell like?

What does the sun smell like? You people. You're odd, but I like you.

Special Report Awards A Gold Star For Ruth Party Reply

January 9, 2000

SPECIAL REPORT: A few weeks ago, students, we gave you a special research assignment: *What is/was a Ruth party?*

At the time, we speculated it may have had something to do with Winnie Ruth Judd, the Valley's famous/infamous trunk murderess. We could not have been more wrong, which is not a remarkably surprising state of affairs.

Actually, we're sort of sorry we asked.

In any event, a big gold star in the *Valley 101 Great Big Book of Life* goes to Marden Chlarson of Mesa, who was the first to provide a "Ruth party" answer. To tell the truth, we didn't believe him at first, but several other students have provided collaborating answers.

This was (and let's hope is no longer) a Ruth party: A group of fun-lovers would find a stranger in town who was looking for a date and one of them, hereafter referred to as Prankster 1, would say he knew a young woman of easy virtue named Ruth whose father was out of town/outside irrigating his crops/otherwise disposed and would offer to make the introduction.

When Prankster 1 and the stranger arrived at "Ruth's home," with other pranksters hidden thereabouts, the "father" would emerge on the porch with a shotgun, cry out, "So you're the one who has been…(use your imagination) with Ruth!" and let go with a shotgun blast.

Prankster 1 and the stranger, of course, fled in terror, mock or otherwise.

After this it gets a bit confusing. Some accounts let the stranger merely run away. Other more complicated plots have him accused of the slaying of Prankster 1, arrested, jailed and threatened with lynching before the joke was revealed.

However it ended, we have to give extra-credit points to the aforementioned Mr. Chlarson, who said, in a classic piece of understatement, "We didn't have a lot to do back then."

Thoughtful? I Think I'll Wait A Day

October 26, 2000

I was playing Hangman on my computer the other day when one of my colleagues stopped by and announced that this space is the "alternative-fuel program" of *Republic* columns.

He might have meant it as a compliment, but he laughed really hard afterward.

Maybe I should be more thoughtful. I now sit between two really serious guys. They are very thoughtful. They are always having thoughtful telephone conversations with other grown-ups about stuff like voter registration trends and equity and Nasdaq.

I suppose they could be pretending to have thoughtful conversations while listening to the time-and-temperature recording, but I don't think so. It sounds very serious, and they frequently wear ties. One of them even has a Rolodex. And I've noticed that my masters never ask either of them to pick up the dry cleaning.

I did do that study once comparing the number of monsoon days in Republican and Democratic administrations. That was pretty thoughtful, don't you think? Kind of added to the civic dialogue, I thought.

Don't you just hate the word "dialogue"? That and "trousers."

Maybe I should call some meteorologists and have thoughtful discussions about barotropic systems or the Beaufort wind scale or something. Or I could call a geologist and have a thoughtful discussion on the effects of schist vs. granite on hiking boots.

Schist is a good word, don't you think? I wonder if geologists ever say stuff like, "I schist got here" and then laugh really hard.

So, it's resolved: From now on, thoughtful. Starting tomorrow. Today's no good. I'm on the verge of a personal-best for consecutive Hangman wins. Then I have to go to the dry cleaner.

Old Boots Best For Cold Bog
October 27, 2000

Ha! Hardly a day's gone by and already things have taken a turn for the thoughtful. No more cheesy jokes and snarky comments here. From now on high-mindedness is the watchword.

As proof I have at hand a letter from an honest-to-goodness geologist on the effects of schist vs. granite on hiking boots. And it is not just any geologist but the estimable Simon Peacock, a professor of geology and chairman — chairman! — of the Department of Geological Sciences at Arizona State University. And he has a Ph.D. And I bet it's in geology. This is pretty upscale for this column, yes?

Dr. Peacock opines thusly on the subject of schist, granite and hiking boots:

"In my opinion, schist (for example, the rocks present on the Squaw Peak trail) is tougher on hiking boots than granite (for example, the rocks that make up the hump of Camelback Mountain). Rot induced by tundra, a fancy word for 'cold bog,' is even tougher on boots."

So, what have we learned here? That the letters in tundra can be rearranged to spell Durant, which is a small town in Iowa. And, you should stay away from cold bogs if you are wearing your good hiking boots.

Ah, It's Good To Be Back In Old Grind

July 3, 2001

Gosh, I can't tell you how good it is to be back. I really just can't tell you.

Nothing much seems to have changed while I was gone. I had no sooner settled my pert butt in my chair than I had a call from a reader who wanted to know if the temperature had ever hit 160 in Phoenix. Really.

Then I took 30 or 40 calls from people who wanted to know what happened to the July weather chart. It turned out nothing happened to the July weather chart. It was in Friday's paper on page B9. You can download a version at www.azcentral.com.

Then I started wading through the e-mail that had piled up over the past week, and, among other things, I found a memo from my masters about some sort of staff reorganization that listed me as Clay Thomas. You know, one thing I like about working here in the Dark Tower is the sort of easygoing atmosphere, the relaxed informality of working directly over a long period of time with respected colleagues who can't remember your last name. It makes you feel that you're not just some cog in a vast, impersonal machine. Instead, you're a cog with somebody else's last name.

Still, coming back to work was a small price to pay for being off last week. It was a pretty good week. One day I took two naps in the same afternoon, a new personal best in sloth. It was great. Aside from that, one of the real highlights of last week came when I found a boogie board that came with a long list of instructions and warnings including this one: "Use Only in Water."

I assume this is for the benefit of people like my masters who, without such a warning, might try to use a boogie board in something like bricks or gasoline.

Coming Wednesday: The winner in the hugely great, big hot-weather limerick contest. I just spoke to him or her and he or she seems very nice and was pleased to be the winner.

One thing: If you don't like the winning limerick, don't blame me. I wasn't the judge. It was that other guy, Clay Thomas.

Hot Weather Stirs Poets Among Us
July 4, 2001

Before we get to the winner of the immensely gargantuan hot-weather limerick contest, let me say a few things about the judging process. Perhaps this will spare some of you the trouble of calling or writing.

Here goes:

Yes, your entry was clearly better. You should have been the winner. I don't know what came over me. You deserved to win and didn't. I'm sorry. I just don't know what I was thinking, but it's too late to change things now.

There. That's that.

There were well over 600 entries, and a lot of them were really, really good. A lot of them were really, really dirty too. You people. Anyway, thanks for entering. It was fun.

There is just enough room for a couple of runners-up. There are no consolation prizes other than the somewhat dubious honor of being printed here.

This also-ran is from Frances Pershing of Mesa:

Her car had a leather interior
'Cause she thought any less was inferior.
She changed her mind when
It reached 110
And the leather seat scorched her posterior.

What do you think? Well, I liked it.

This close-but-no-cigar is from Wendy Clay of Phoenix:

Last summer, despite my rebuke,
My cousin (out here from Dubuque)
Ran up like a streak
To the top of Squaw Peak.
Since then we've called it Squaw Puke.

Not bad, not bad, but unfortunately we can only have one winner. And the prize — two tickets to the Diamondbacks-Padres game July 23 — goes to Jane Malcolm, who lives in Scottsdale but has the good sense to spend her summers in Heber. Here it is:

Old Scratch, on a hot Valley mission.
Said, "Why promise folks wealth and position?
With their smog and their heat
They'll see hell as a treat.
For it's cooler back home in Perdition.

See? I told you yours was better.

Clap For Me If I Become A Warlord

January 12, 2002

I'm thinking of becoming a warlord. No particular reason, other than you hear the word a lot lately, and it sounds kind of cool.

I'm not exactly sure what warlording involves, but I suppose I could find out. It would certainly be a way to impress people you meet at parties or wherever. "Me? Oh, I'm a warlord. Yeah, I was in newspapers for a while, and then I got into the warlording game. I guess I'm just a people person."

Most of the warlords you see have rocket-powered grenade launchers. That might be a problem. Maybe I could just get a big stick.

I'll have to look into this. Meanwhile, we shall take up today's question:

What is the origin of clapping as a sign of pleasure or appreciation?

Nobody knows for sure, but people probably have been clapping ever since they freed up their hands by walking on two legs. Other than speech, it is about the most basic sound-making tool we have, and it doesn't make you hoarse. Early people probably clapped to signal the group while hunting or whatever.

Go outside and experiment to see which can be heard at the greatest distance — a shout or a sharp clap. Never mind the neighbors. They're probably used to you by now.

Clapping as a sign of appreciation or joy is as old as the Bible. Psalm 47 says "Clap your hands, all peoples, shout to God with the voice of joy."

Clapping was also a sign of disapproval. In Job it says, "Men shall clap their hands at him and shall hiss him out of his place."

One theory I found said clapping is a symbolic hug, because you are extending your hands and arms in sort of the same way you would if you were going to give someone a big squeeze.

Clapping can mean different things in different cultures.

In Tibet people clap to drive away evil spirits. I've tried this on my masters, but it only seems to confuse them.

Wrong Mold Can Leave You Feeling Blue
February 7, 2002

Why is the mold in blue cheese OK to eat while the mold that grows on other food in the refrigerator isn't?

I am taking up this question, even though it involves a number of words that are hard to spell, because I am deeply fond of blue cheese.

In fact, I have a secret stash of Maytag blue cheese that I take out only late at night when I am alone and have pulled all the drapes and double-locked the doors.

In the course of researching this question I came across the instructions for making your own blue cheese, but it takes two months of almost steady monitoring and for some reason involves a Philips screwdriver. I'll stick to the store-bought.

The answer is really fairly simple. There are all sorts of molds and all sorts of bacteria.

They can be roughly broken down into two categories, which, without getting too technical, we shall call the good molds and bacteria and the naughty molds and bacteria.

In a nutshell, the good ones don't hurt us and may even be good for us, while the bad ones make us sick or even kill us. Well, duh.

Most blue cheeses are made by introducing a mold into the curds of one kind of milk or another. The mold is various strains of *penicillium glaucum.*

These strains are, of course, related to the stuff that gives us penicillin. For some reason people who are allergic to penicillin are rarely allergic to blue cheeses.

Some other good guys include *lactobacillus bulgaricus* and *streptococcus thermophilus*, in yogurt, and *lactobacillus sanfrancisco* in sourdough bread.

Then there are the naughty ones, the ones that will have you up all night talking to Rolf on the big white phone. They include stuff like *clostridium botulinum* — botulism — and salmonella. There is a fungus that grows on some grains known as vomitoxin because it makes pigs barf, which, if you think about it, probably takes some doing.

Blame Irish, Not Scots, For Bagpipes

March 12, 2002

Why are bagpipes played at police funerals? Is there some Scottish police connection that I don't know about?

I used to have a recording of bagpipe music that I played at great volume to wake my children up in the morning.

Once.

It mysteriously disappeared after that.

Most of us associate bagpipes with Scotland, but, in fact, the pipes as we know them are an Irish instrument. In other forms, they are traced back as far as 4000 B.C. In Genesis 4:21, Jubal is referred to as "the ancestor of those who play the harp and pipe," and there are people who will tell you that meant bagpipes. I don't know.

The Irish are believed to have carried the bagpipe to Scotland sometime around 470 during one war or another. Traditionally, the Irish version has two drones, one bass and one tenor, and the Scottish version has one bass and two tenors.

Bagpipes are, of course, associated with battles and wars and the martial spirit in general. In some Irish laws enacted around 400, pipes are referred to as *cuisle*, which meant pulse, as in the blood pulsing your veins. But they also were used at weddings, dances and funerals, especially heroes' funerals. I could make some cheesy joke here about waking the dead, but I'll pass.

When the Irish started coming to America in big numbers and settling in the big East Coast cities, they faced a lot of discrimination, that whole "No Irish need apply" thing. So they ended up with a lot of jobs nobody much wanted, such as police and fire work.

Since they had brought the pipes with them, it was only natural that they played them at funerals.

The tradition spread, and now the bagpipes seem to be played at almost every funeral for a police officer or firefighter, Irish, Scottish or whatever.

Scratching, Spitting: It's A Guy Thing
May, 20, 2002

Today we have two questions relating to the mannerisms of professional athletes. I have painstakingly researched these matters by wandering over to ask sports columnist Dan Bickley about them and then going to the cafeteria to see if there was any pie.

The first question:

Why do baseball players scratch and spit so much?

Because they are guys.

As for scratching, baseball players wear protective cups, which, while not onerous, are not always especially comfortable. From time to time — digging in at the plate, for instance — a player will find it necessary to sort of rearrange matters.

As for spitting, many baseball players are or have been users of chewing tobacco, which, of course, requires spitting. So they spit, either out of necessity or habit. Since Major League Baseball discourages the use of smokeless tobacco, many players now use bubble gum or sunflower seeds, which also involve some spitting.

All this expectorating is not especially attractive, but it is no worse than watching some guy at a traffic light who opens the car door and hacks a big old phloogey all over the street. Ewww.

Second question:

My wife and I disagree on the bathing and shaving habits of male athletes. I have noted that many of them are not clean-shaven during the game. Why should they shower or shave before playing? My wife feels that everyone, in competition or just working out, should first prepare themselves by showering and shaving.

Let's face it: Your wife is a girl.

Bickley confirmed that the vast majority of athletes shower and shave after the game and not before. However, he did say that when he was covering the Chicago Bulls, he noticed that Dennis Rodman would finish the game, spend some time on an exercise bike and then dress and head out for a night on the town without showering.

See "ewww" above.

Cleavage Question Toes The Line

June 1, 2002

In keeping with Valley 101's reputation for living on the cutting edge of style, fashion and weirdness in general, we take up the following question:

Recently I was on the elevator with two women who were discussing what they should wear to some event they were planning to attend, and one of them said, "Those shoes have too much toe cleavage for something like this." Why haven't I ever heard of toe cleavage before?

Because you are not a groovy hepcat like me, daddy-o.

I shall explain directly, but first let me tell you that in the course of researching this matter, I discovered there are Web sites for guys who get turned on by plush stuffed toys. Also, there are Web sites for guys who get turned on by pictures of girls sinking in quicksand. How weird is that? There is also something called a body inflation fetish, which you don't want to know about. And why is it always guys who have these weird fetish things going and not women?

Anyway, toe cleavage is the amount of toe that a woman shows when wearing open-toed shoes. The more toe that is showing, the more alluring it is meant to be.

It doesn't come into play with shoes that expose the full length of the toe.

I discussed this matter with Nancy Baca, our fashion writer, who seemed to be fingering her pepper-spray dispenser while we talked. She said there are not a lot of dress-code kind of rules about this, although she did say that maybe a funeral, for instance, would not be an appropriate place to be airing out a lot of toe flesh.

The idea, according to Baca, is that if you have big feet you want to show a lot of toe because it makes your feet look smaller.

Apparently toe cleavage is not a sexual sort of thing as such unless, I suppose, you are really into toes. Personally, I prefer the more traditional body parts and the more traditional major muscle groups, but if you like toes, it's no business of mine.

Hats In Air, Souvenirs For The Kids

June 4, 2002

After Saturday's column on toe cleavage, a number of you called or sent e-mail to report that toe cleavage refers not to the space between all the toes but only the gap between the big toe and the second toe. Apparently, the more of this gap that shows, the more attractive it is meant to be.

Fine.

This brings to a close the brief but glorious toe cleavage chapter in Valley 101's long and dubious history. It is time to move on.

So what shall we talk about today? Nuclear war between India and Pakistan? Terrorism? Farm subsidies? Unrest in the Middle East?

Nah.

Let us consider this instead:

After graduation ceremonies at military academies, you always see pictures of the graduating cadets throwing their hats in the air. How do they find their own hats afterward in that big jumble of headwear? I've asked a lot of my friends about this, and they just stare at me.

Sometimes people ask me if I am ever embarrassed to call up experts and ask them dumb questions. There is no such thing as a dumb question. There are just a lot of inquisitive silly people. And, besides, after you work for newspapers for a while, your threshold of embarrassment is pretty high.

I put this matter to Joyce Powell, a public affairs person at the U.S. Air Force Academy in Colorado Springs where the cadets were throwing their hats in the air just the other day. She did not seem to think it was a dumb question or, if she did, she didn't say so.

"Before the hat-throwing ceremony, they let the children in the audience come down on the field and they run after the hats," Powell said.

Since the hats are part of their cadet uniforms, the new officers don't need them anymore, and the kids get to keep them as souvenirs.

Now tell your friends to stop staring at you. It's not polite.

When Jokes Aren't Quite So Humorous

June 16, 2002

One day, several years ago, he and the younger girl and the father were home together, and a drywall man came to the house to do some work.

The drywall man was cheerful and friendly, and he liked dogs. But when the father stepped out in the yard for a minute and left him and the girl and drywall man alone in the house, the dog got up and ambled over to the drywall man, who was pretty much minding his own business, and bit him. Then he ambled back and sat down by the girl.

It was really just a nip, mostly just to tell the drywall man that despite his looks he was pretty much ferocious and that he had his eye on the drywall man and had his eye on the girl, and if the drywall man knew what was good for him, he should just keep drywalling.

He was just bluffing. As the older girl said later, he always had a good sense of humor. He liked a good joke.

He was in his prime then and in charge of things. He was in charge of drywall men and tennis balls and boyfriends and the kitchen wastebasket and poorly guarded birthday cakes. He was in charge of barking at stuff and of looking under the covers during storms to make sure anyone else under there was OK. He was in charge of the younger girl and the older girl, and after things changed, he was in charge of their mother, too.

When he was 17 and it came time to go to the vet for the last time, he wasn't much in charge of anything. He was purely worn out.

Before they went to the vet that time, the mother and the father and the older girl sat by him on the floor where he didn't feel like doing anything much other than resting his head on a pillow. They talked to him, and they talked to each other, and the story about the drywall man came up, and he lifted his head up off the pillow at that and gave them all a smile.

He always did like a good joke.

Feet, So Don't Have A Cow
August 4, 2002

One thing I like about having you people around is that you remind me about stuff I keep putting off or forgetting to do.

For instance, I have been meaning to look up the answer to today's question since I was 8 years old. I just never got around to it until now.

My son rubs his baseball glove with neat's-foot oil. What exactly is it anyway? Did a lot of neats have their feet cut off so my son could break in his glove?

Neat's-foot oil is a pale yellow oil that is made by boiling the hooves and shinbones of cattle, horses, sheep or pigs and skimming the oil off the surface of the water. That doesn't sound like much fun, does it?

It is widely used for treating leather and also for canning sardines. Don't ask me why they use it for canning sardines.

I don't know, and I don't like sardines anyway.

Neat is an archaic Norse or Old English word for bovines, specifically cattle. As in:

"He a high altar made me of heaped stones/all glary have grown the gathered rocks/and reddened anew them with neats' fresh blood/For ay believed Ottar in the asynjur." Don't ask me who Ottar was or what an asynjur is. I don't know. It's Norse or something.

Neat hasn't been used in the cattle sense since the 12th century, but don't you think it's kind of cool that it hangs on still today in the form of neat's-foot oil?

Debating the best way to break in a baseball glove is a major guy thing. I'd never heard of this one before, but I am told that shaving cream that contains lanolin is a cheap alternative to neat's-foot oil.

Apparently what you do is put a dab of shaving cream on a cloth and knead it into the mitt, working outward from the palm until you've coated the whole glove.

Let it dry overnight and then play catch for a while so the glove conforms to the shape of the kid's hand. Then put a ball in the pocket, tie it up with a string or rubber band and let it sit for two days.

A postscript: No neats were harmed in the production of this column.

Boldly Going Where Few Men Dare
August 9, 2002

As you know, Valley 101 is a full-service column, willing to take on, without hesitation, any question that doesn't require much work to answer.

Hence, today we boldly stride into a new frontier for Valley 101 — ladies clothes.

Everyone knows that horizontal stripes make a person look bigger around. This is OK for men, but horizontal stripes on a woman's T-shirt or blouse make her look fat. Why are the stripes always horizontal instead of vertical, which would be slimming?

For starters, let us bear in mind that you're asking someone who does most of his clothes shopping at yard sales. So for help with this matter I turned to a panel of experts selected from a pool of people who know more about fashion than I do, which would be every woman in the world. In other words, I walked around the newsroom awhile and asked some females about this.

This was not as productive as I had hoped because most of them pretended they were talking on the phone when they saw me coming. However, the consensus seems to be that vertical stripes are hard to find, but they're around if you look hard enough.

Not content with this paltry advice, I turned for help to that international arbiter of fashion, the online edition of *The Hindu*, which bills itself as India's national paper. There I learned — ladies, you might want to get a paper and pencil and write this down — that diagonal stripes are very big these days. They can, according to *The Hindu*, make you look taller and thinner.

And, as a fashion bonus, I also learned in the course of my research why black pants make your butt look smaller or at least not as big as it really is.

It's because we only perceive shapes by means of different colors or shades. If you're wearing white pants, the shape of your butt is discerned by the slight shadows cast by the contours of that particular body part. If you are wearing black, the shadows don't show.

Or, as they say in Rome, *"No, non penso che marche che del vestito sembrate grassi,"* which is Italian for "No, I don't think that dress makes you look fat."

Putting A Finger On Obscene Origin

August 28, 2002

I have been thinking about your funeral. I attended a large memorial service recently, and the next day happened to be talking to a friend who had also been there, and he said the deceased really would have enjoyed the whole proceeding.

So I'm thinking, why can't we have our funerals while we're still alive? You could do it when you were getting old and starting to feel like maybe the end was in sight. That way you could hear all the nice things people say about you in the eulogies and hear everybody say how much they're going to miss you and what a swell person you were. Then you could all go out for a big lunch.

Just an idea. I need to refine it a bit. In the meantime, we shall consider today's question.

What is the origin of using the middle finger as an obscene gesture?

There is a legend that at the Battle of Agincourt in 1415, the French threatened to cut off the middle fingers of the English archers, leaving them unable to draw a bowstring properly. When the English won, they taunted the French by waving their middle fingers.

I have not read such hooey since the last time my masters sent out a staff memo.

Flipping the bird is an ancient custom whose roots are unknown. It goes all the way back to ancient Greece.

The earliest known reference to the middle finger as an obscene gesture is in Aristophanes' play *The Clouds*, which probably came out around 420 B.C. It's in a dialogue between Socrates and one of his students, which I am not going to repeat here in the interest of good taste.

The Finger was widely used as a gesture of contempt by the Romans. In Latin, it was known as the *digitus impudicus* — the impudent or dirty finger.

While we're on the subject, do you know why your middle finger is longer than the others? Neither does anyone else.

Here's one theory: When you close your hand to make a fist or grab something, all the fingers touch the palm at the same time. So if you are grabbing a vine or a club or whatever, the fingers are sharing the workload equally.

Works for me.

The Trick To Great Halloween Treats
October 29, 2002

Do you have your Halloween costume ready? I hope so, because it's getting too late to put together something really elaborate, and just a sheet with eye holes cut out is going to look sort of lame.

I'm going as a hobo, but then that's the same costume I use every year. It's easy because all it requires is a stick with a bundle tied on the end and the same clothes I'd be wearing anyway.

Let me know if you are giving popcorn balls or little boxes of raisins to trick-or-treaters. That way I'll know to avoid your place. On the other hand, if you are giving out pie or money, call right away with directions to your house.

I like Halloween a lot, mostly because one of my smart and good-looking daughters was born on Halloween but also because people really get into it and sit around and think up questions such as this:

My co-workers and I are wondering why black and orange are the traditional colors of Halloween?

Orange is easy. Duh. Orange is an autumn kind of color. Harvest moons, pumpkins, fall leaves, fading embers, bad dye jobs and so on.

Black is a little more complicated. Obviously, Halloween is associated with the night, but there is more to it than that, depending on how silly you want to get about it.

Most people agree that Halloween goes back to the ancient Celtic celebration of *Samhain*, which was the beginning of winter and, in a nutshell, an important religious holiday that had a lot to do with the spirit world.

To the ancient Celtics, black was the presence of all light and therefore sacred and readily associated with a major date like Samhain. To the Christians, who turned Samhain into the Eve of All Saints, or All Hallows Day, black is associated with death and spirits and evil and so on.

So you can make whatever you want out of black as a color of Halloween. I wouldn't get too worked up about it if I were you. Just have fun and hope your kids get a lot of those little Snickers or Milky Ways that you can snarf up when they're not looking.

They can always eat the popcorn balls.

Here's A Kiss For Your Nose
February 13, 2003

MAJOR NEWS FLASH: Drop everything and go to the store right now and buy a bag of those Hershey's Kisses things.

Actually, you should probably get two bags. This might take some practice.

This would not be a matter of such urgency if it were not for the fact that Friday is Valentine's Day, and this involves traditional Valentine's Day issues such as chocolate and kisses and assorted body parts.

I learned of this matter the other day just after I had finished a column on your tongue, but then it was too late to include this vital information in that piece. You know, running into the newsroom late at night waving a bag of Hershey's Kisses and yelling, "Stop the presses!" just doesn't have the impact you might think it would. At least the security guards were nice enough about it.

OK, before we go on: I have to tell you that I, my own personal self, have not yet actually tried this, although I intend to as soon I get back from the store with some more Kisses. So, in all honesty, at the moment I am not actually sure how hard it is to do this or what side effects may be involved.

And neither I nor my employers nor their employers nor our advertisers nor your newspaper carrier nor anyone who may have even glanced at today's newspaper takes any responsibility or liability or accountability or any of your other major -bilities if you try this and then end up in a care home wearing Depends and living on beef broth because you have a Hershey's Kiss wedged in some especially useful and inoperable part of your brain.

OK?

So anyway, this is what you do (this is so cool): Unwrap a Hershey's Kiss and put it in your mouth for a couple of seconds to kind of soften it up. Take it out of your mouth. Extend your tongue. Balance the Hershey's Kiss on the tip of your tongue.

Now, flick your tongue up so the Hershey's Kiss shoots up and lodges in one of your nostrils. Again, I haven't actually tried this yet.

However, I am reliably told that seeing someone else shoot a Hershey's Kiss up his or her nose is extremely humorous.

And just imagine the heights of delight — nay, even passion — to which your sweet patootie will be elevated when he or she gazes on the sight of you with a tear-drop-shaped piece of chocolate stuck in your nose. Maybe even two pieces, one in each nostril, if you are especially gifted, tongue-wise.

I guarantee you that if you pull this off, this will be a Valentine's Day your sweetheart will never forget, even after years of therapy.

Helping Toast Know If It's Toast

February 22, 2003

You would not believe how long it took me to find the answer to today's question. It came dangerously close to involving actual work, something I believe I have talked to you people about before. Let's try to be more careful in the future, shall we?

Every morning I arise, let the dog out, feed the cat and then make my coffee and a slice of toast. This morning, for some reason, I noticed the inscription on the toaster "single slice here" with an arrow pointing to the right-hand slot. Why is that?

Did you know there actually are people who collect toasters? Toasters? Did you know a Universal model E9410 push-button toaster from the 1920s is going to cost you around $1,500? Did you know there is a Toaster Museum Foundation (www.toaster.org) that is trying to raise $30,000 to open a toaster museum? Do you find this a bit odd? I do, but then I guess if people want to collect toasters it really isn't any of my business.

Now before we start on the answer: There are toasters and there are toasters. Some toasters, indeed, will not work if you put just a single slice in the other slot, the one not designated for single slices. Some will. If yours is one that works in either slot, that's nice, but it is not necessary to call and tell me about it. I'm sure it would be charming to talk to you, but frankly toasters hold little appeal for me.

A toaster is a fairly simple device. A spring-loaded tray lowers the bread and triggers the heating elements that cook the bread with radiant heat. A timer, or the browning control, turns off the elements when the time is up. The rack is released by an electromagnetic catch and up pops your toast.

If you like, we could pause to discuss the Maillard reaction in which heat causes sugars and starches in bread to caramelize and take on new flavors. That, however, would probably just confuse things.

I did find one explanation of this single-slice thing that involved the behavior of electrons, but it made my brain hurt so I threw it out.

Here is a more likely explanation: In some toasters, there is a sensor, like a thermostat or something, that determines when toast is toast.

In some toasters that sensor is on the side of the single-slice slot, and it probably also is on the same side as the darkness control knob.

If you put your bread in the other slot and there is nothing in the single-slice slot for the sensor to read, chances are your toast isn't going to come out the way you like it, and your morning and maybe even your entire day will be ruined.

Unleashing The Zipper Monopoly
March 28, 2003

The other night over dinner and some wine, my wife bet me a week of doing the dishes and all the laundry that at least half the zippers on my clothes would have the letters YKK on the zipper tab. An hour later, after going through all my clothes, I was doomed to a week of dishes and laundry. What's the deal? Is YKK something left over from Y2K?

A few things here:

First: It took you an hour to look at the zippers on all your clothes? How many zippers do you have, for heaven's sake?

Second: That was a sucker's bet. Especially since wine was involved. You should have gone with Scrabble instead. My parents used to play Scrabble every night after supper to see who had to do the dishes. That's why the old man died with dishpan hands. And, by the way, if you had played "zippers" on a triple-word score, it would have been worth 110 points, enough to keep you away from the sink or the washing machine for weeks.

Third: No, YKK is not something related to Y2K. Duh. I'm sorry, but if you fell for a bet like that, you deserve a duh.

YKK is short for Yoshida Kogyo Kabushikikaisha. It's pronounced like it's spelled. Maybe. I don't really know. It is the name of a company based in Japan that pretty much dominates the zipper industry.

It opened for business in 1934 but later changed its name to just plain YKK, because, I'm thinking, the whole Yoshida Kogyo Kabushikikaisha thing was pretty hard to fit on the tab of a zipper. YKK has come over the years to pretty much dominate the zipper business.

Don't you think that's kind of cool? That somewhere at sometime some person — Mr. Kabushukikaisha, perhaps? — hit upon an idea for getting rich by dominating the zipper business, an idea that would never have occurred to the rest of us in a thousand years? Well, I think it's cool.

Anyway, YKK has zipper factories in something like more than 200 countries, and each of those zipperoriums — I made that up — produces up to 7 million zippers a day, cloth, dyed cloth, brass works and all. Seven million zippers a day. That would be something to go home and tell the kids about, don't you think?

As long as we are on the subject, a guy named Whitcomb Judson first came up with the idea of the zipper in 1893 as a way of helping a friend who couldn't button up his shoes because he had a bad back. He called it the "hookless fastener."

The idea didn't really take off until several years later when the Goodrich Co. started using hookless fasteners on galoshes — remember galoshes? — and they closed up with a zip. Hence, zipper.

A History Lesson On Black Tires
April 28, 2003

I have here a question from a gentleman who wants to know about homosexuality among ducks.

Pass.

Instead: *My 18-year-old son wants to know why tires are always black and don't come in colors.*

Colored tires? That would be kind of weird, wouldn't it?

OK, first of all, I don't know, but I would not be at all surprised to find out that if you looked hard enough among automobile specialty or customizing magazines or Web sites, you might actually be able to find colored tires. I am not planning on looking through such resources myself because I do not want to have colored tires.

Next, in the late 1990s, BF Goodrich did come out with a line of performance tires with stripes of color in the tread. You had your pick of two colors, Raging Red or Screaming Yellow.

None of the other tire companies followed suit and the stripes did not catch on. I'm not sure if people just didn't like them or what. I couldn't get a hold of the Goodrich people to find out.

Now back in the old, old days, tires were not necessarily black. They were made from rubber that was sort of tan by nature. Of course, they showed the dirt pretty well, but then they were tires, weren't they? They were supposed to be dirty.

Anyway, according to Dan Zielinski, a spokesman for the Rubber Manufacturers Association in Washington, D.C., sooner or later the tire people discovered a substance called carbon black that would, fittingly so, make tires black.

What is carbon black? It's a petroleum derivative, a very pure, light, powdery form of carbon, and it accounts for around 30 percent of the stuff that goes into most tires.

So, it turned out the carbon black not only turned tires black, but it dramatically increased their structural strength. One source I found said that tires made with carbon black are about five times more durable than the old tan-colored tires.

Another source compared carbon black in tires to rebar in concrete.

And in addition to strengthening the tire, it protects from the sun's ultraviolet rays, which can break down rubber molecules.

The thing about this wonderful carbon black is that it is black and cannot be made to be anything other than black. Apparently, you can't dye the stuff.

Over the years, Zielinski said, tire manufacturers have experimented with other substances that would be as strong and durable as carbon black and that could be dyed, but so far they haven't come up with anything.

Cry 'Pez!' And Wreak Havoc
May 29, 2003

Someone just called and asked if I could get a branch library placed in their neighborhood. I'm afraid something like that would cut way too deeply into my crossword time, not to mention watching baseball games. Sorry.

Let's turn to today's question instead:

I am curious about the phrase "to wreak havoc." Can havoc be anything other than wreaked? And can anything else except havoc be wreaked?

Let's say, just hypothetically speaking, that the person who asked this question is someone you really wanted to impress and someone that you suspect thinks you're an idiot, and when the question is presented you suddenly blurt out, "Sure, you could say, 'The garbage reeks,'" or something like that even though you know the difference between wreaks and reeks perfectly well.

So, just hypothetically mind you, does that make you a moron?

Don't answer that.

Havoc and wreak — which of course is pronounced reek — are both pretty good words, and they are both pretty old words.

Wreak comes from the Old English word *wrecan*, meaning to punish or avenge. Wrecan goes back to wreg-, the Indo-European root for push or shove.

Wreak is sort of related to the words wrack and wreck. See how many times you can say "wrack, wreck, wreak" really fast. Now try it with crackers in your mouth.

Havoc probably traces back to the Old French word *havot*, meaning to hook or to take.

Anyway, the answer is yes, stuff other than havoc can be wreaked, and havoc's possibilities are not limited only to being wreaked. (A lot of people, incidentally, think the past tense of wreak is wrought. It isn't.)

For one thing, havoc can be cried. So in Julius Caesar, Shakespeare writes: "Cry 'Havoc!' and let slip the dogs of war." It means to start pillaging or looting and otherwise carrying on.

I think havoc can be raised, although I'm not sure. It definitely can be played, as in, "Constantly having to stop and show my masters how to work a Pez dispenser plays havoc with my routine."

Nor is wreaking limited to havoc. Vengeance gets wreaked quite a bit, and every now and then destruction gets wreaked, too. As in, "Even while the storm was wreaking destruction on the city, my masters were bugging me about their Pez dispensers."

Even though they are both old words, one source I found said the first person to use the phrase "wreak havoc" was Agatha Christie in 1923.

That sounds a little odd to me, but who knows?

At least she didn't write "reek havoc."

Re: Chili: Bean There, Done That

November 14, 2003

A friend of mine and I are having a disagreement on the origins of chili. I say chili came from Mexico and contains chile peppers and beans. She says chili originated in the Southwest and contains chile peppers and meat. Can you let us know which one of us is correct?

We had a chili-cooking contest at church a few years ago, and I won a special prize for being the worst loser. It was a purple ribbon with a rosette. I still have it somewhere. I only mention it because I think it's important to celebrate our successes, don't you?

Actually, I only mentioned it to kill time because I am trying to put off dealing with this meat vs. beans thing. Some people tend to get a little overwrought when discussing this issue, and I know no matter what I say, I'm going to spend the next week or so listening to you people complain about it.

Let's start at the beginning. Chile peppers are native to the Amazon region and early on spread through various Native American cultures.

Of course, chiles aren't really pepper, like the stuff on your table. That kind of pepper was one of the things Columbus was on his way to the Orient to buy when he ran into the New World. Apparently, he tried some chiles and figured, what the heck, he'd just call them peppers anyway.

As for the origins of chili, it's hard to say.

There are plenty of accounts of Native Americans in Mexico and the Southwest eating various types of stew flavored with chile peppers. The Aztec emperor Montezuma is said to have eaten a plate of chiles first thing every morning, which certainly would get your blood flowing, although I think I'll stick with oatmeal.

It's seems pretty likely, although not certain, that your friend is right about chili being a Southwestern thing and not Mexican. I found one chili Web site that claimed that until recently the definition of chili in the *Diccionario de Mejicanismos* was "detestable food passing itself off as Mexican, sold in the U.S.," but since I don't happen to have a copy of the *Diccionario de Mejicanismos* at hand, I don't know if that is true.

What we think of as chili probably originated with cowboys who had plenty of beef around and could always find some wild onions and chile peppers to throw in the stew.

Or, if you are of the bean school, what we think of as chili probably got its start as a kind of bean stew with some chile peppers added to brighten it up a bit.

OK, now — beans or meat? Here's my bold stand. Only weenies make chili with...Oh, look, we're out of space. Dang. I guess you guys will just have to decide about it yourselves.

Dogs, Cats And French Onion Soup
February 28, 2004

I just read a wire story about a fifth-grade girl in North Dakota who won a prize at her school science fair for proving that dog slobber has more germs in it than cat slobber. I mentioned this to my cat, who gave me a look that suggested any fool would know that. Of course, it's the same look the cat always gives me.

Anyway, isn't that a great idea for a science fair project? I thought so. I think they should give her another prize just for thinking of the idea in the first place. Maybe some day I could hire her as my assistant. Meanwhile, I shall soldier on alone in dealing with today's question.

I have never received an answer for this other than "Blame the French." If a major outranks a lieutenant, why does a lieutenant general outrank a major general? "Blame the French" is not a good answer.

I don't see why not. I'm sure there's a lot of stuff we could blame on the French. For example, if the French, our so-called friends, had only spoken up before we invaded Iraq, we might not be in this mess. Oh, wait, they did speak up, didn't they? Never mind. But I bet there's plenty of other stuff that's their fault. French onion soup. Actually, I like French onion soup, but it's hard to eat because the cheese gets all stringy.

Anyway, about the question: It's a good thing I hadn't thrown out my copy of the December 1967 edition of *Army Digest* because it included an article by one Charles F. Romanus all about the origins of military ranks.

The word "lieutenant" comes to us from those pesky French people from the Latin words *locum teneris*, meaning "holding in place of." So if there isn't a captain handy, the lieutenant acts in his or her place. And "major" comes from the Latin *magnus*, meaning "something greater." And the word "sergeant" — follow along here — comes from a Latin legal phrase and more or less means servant.

Some European armies once included a rank of sergeant-major-general, which would've roughly meant "a bigger servant to a general." The "sergeant" part fell away from the title over time.

Let's review what we've learned so far: A lieutenant would be someone acting in the place of someone else. A (sergeant) major would be someone acting as an important servant to someone else.

Hence, etymologically speaking, a lieutenant general may act for a general while a major general would serve the general, and hence, a lieutenant general outranks a major general. Or, as the saying goes, *Veuillez demander a votre chien de cesser de radoter sur moi*, which is French for "please ask your dog to stop drooling on me."

Billy Is A Devil Of A Name
March 11, 2004

My grandfather used to use the expression "all billy hell." He'd say something like, "It rained like all billy hell" or, "He went out of there faster than all billy hell." I never asked him what it meant, and I've always wondered about it.

Your grandfather said "all billy hell"? No kidding? So did my dad. I wonder if we're related. That would be weird, huh, if we were related. Not that it would be weird to be related to you, but it would be weird if we found out we were related because we both knew people who said that. Well, it might be weird to be related to you. I don't know. Genetics can be a tricky business.

Anyway, I haven't heard anybody say "billy hell" in years. I never asked my dad about the expression, either, mostly because he used it only when he was fairly well aggravated, and when he was fairly well aggravated, he didn't tend to be in the mood to discuss etymology.

So, in memory of the old man, I actually spent some time on this one, and, as is so often the case, the answer is fuzzy. Billy, of course, has been used as a nickname for William for centuries. Don't ask me how that came to be. I don't know.

This much is pretty certain: Billy hell is related to the British or maybe Irish or maybe Scottish expression "billy-o," which the dictionary says is an intensifier and means energetically, forcefully, rapidly and so on.

It's possible billy-o comes from the Rev. Joseph Billio, who was a 17th-century English minister known for packing them into the pews with his fiery sermons. Hence the expression "like billio." Or it might have something to do with William (Billy) III, who thumped King James II and his Irish allies at a battle in Ireland in 1690.

However, since the expression "billy-o" didn't turn up in the printed word until about two centuries after William III or Joseph Billio, both those explanations seem kind of unlikely.

So I found an etymology feature called "World Wide Words" by a guy named Michael Quinion that included some of these ideas and also offered a fairly plausible explanation for billy-o or billy hell, which

I will now steal and try to make it sound like it was something I already knew because I am so smart.

As far back as Shakespearean times, there were many expressions involving billy as a euphemism for the devil, such as "billy-be-damned" or possibly even "billy hell" itself. So to go like billy hell or to go like billy-o would mean to go like the devil, which, one assumes, is energetically, forcefully or rapidly.

Afterword

This is the second year in a row I have scammed Bill and Amanda Fessler of Primer Publishers into putting out a collection of Valley 101 columns. The first one was called *Valley 101: A Slightly Skewed Guide to Living in Arizona*. Or something like that. I thought it was kind of a dopey title until I remembered it was my idea to begin with. You can still find a copy of it — or even hundreds of copies of it — at a fine book store near you. Or in the trunk of the Fesslers' car.

So this is the second one. I think after this one maybe I should give it a rest for a couple of years until things blow over. We'll see. It depends on how good the publishers' memories are. In any event, it might be a while before we do another one.

So maybe you should buy two copies in case one gets lost or stolen or set on fire or you shoot it by accident or something like that.

And don't forget the incredible Valley 101 bobblehead doll, available at fine stores or yard sales near you now. No home should be without one. Or two. They may even be collectors items some day, depending on how far our cultural standards drop.

You can order another copy of either book or the bobblehead doll — or even a case of them — by visiting www.claythompsonbooks.com or calling 800-521-9221. If computers and phones aren't your thing, you can always write to Primer Publishers, 5738 N. Central Ave., Phoenix, AZ 85012 and ask for a catalog of Clay's Great Stuff, not that there actually is such a catalog. Trust me, they'll be happy to take your money and send me what they laughingly call my fair share.